About the Author

Jeroninio (Jerry) Almeida prefers his favorite title 'Just Another Volunteer'. Besides working as a volunteer and social crusader, Jerry is also a celebrated teacher; inspirational orator; life, performance, executive & success coach; UN advisor and storyteller. Besides creating the *Karma Kurry* book series, Jerry is also soon launching the moJOsh Inspirator book series for enabling people for self-discovery and development through his research and learning that has benefited people around the world. In 2016, Jerry was commissioned by the Prime Minister's Office (PMO) and a publishing house to co-author the book, *Mann Ki Baat*, with Rajendran Panickar, on Honorable Prime Minister of India Narendra Modi's interaction with the masses. More details about Jerry are on www.jerrylearns2learn.com

"[These stories] have that power to inspire people to rise and act, to make a difference."

~ Nelson Mandela

"I am extremely encouraged and inspired with all your Karma Kurry stories and the thoughts in your moJOsh Leadership learning notes, which you shared with me for my feedback. To encapsulate my feedback for the learning on the moJOsh Inspirator notes, I simply have a dozen words 'The learning is awe-inspiring and simply potent to positively impact all humankind.'"

~ Dr. APJ Abdul Kalam,
Scientist & Former Indian President

"When Jerry presents his stories and thoughts, one gets insights from thousands of books, places, people and villages."

~ Amartya Sen, Nobel Laureate, Economist and Author

"The book is so gripping because it is not a story of crime grime and sorrow, but of happiness and joy derived from giving. I continued to read the unique, inspiring and awesome stories of the unsung heroes, not least the story of the author of the book, and the thought came to my mind at well after midnight, 'This book may change my identity after all.'"

~ Dr. Ela Gandhi, Peace Activist &
Former Member of Parliament, South Africa

"I like the Karma and Right every Wrong mission that balances ethical whistle blowing with telling stories of real heroes to inspire change champions and voices of dissent to challenge status quo."

~ Noam Chomsky, Political Commentator & Author

""These heroic stories must be read by all children and youth in schools, colleges and Universities."

~ Philip Zimbardo, Founder of the Heroic Imagination
Project and living legend known for his Stanford Prison
Experiment, Lucifer Effect

BOOK 2

KARMA
KURRY
for the *hero* in *me*

Ordinary People Extraordinary Deeds

JERONINIO (JERRY) ALMEIDA

JAICO PUBLISHING HOUSE

Ahmedabad Bangalore Bhopal Bhubaneswar Chennai
Delhi Hyderabad Kolkata Lucknow Mumbai

Published by Jaico Publishing House
A-2 Jash Chambers, 7-A Sir Phirozshah Mehta Road
Fort, Mumbai - 400 001
jaicopub@jaicobooks.com
www.jaicobooks.com

© Jeroninio Almeida

KARMA KURRY FOR THE HERO IN ME
ISBN 978-93-86348-13-5

First Jaico Impression: 2017

Page design and layout: Special Effects, Mumbai

To my loving father Wilfred Simon Almeida
who became one with the universe on December 16, 1978,
and motivating step-father Bevin Lawrence Martins who
joined my father and other heavenly stars on June 5, 2014.
My gratitude for all your positive contributions in my life.

Contents

Author's Note

Dear Friends and Fellow moJOsh Inspirators,

Namaste! The God in me respects the God in you, the divinity in me salutes the divinity in you and the heroic potential in me recognizes the heroic potential in you. This, my friends, is what the word Namaste fundamentally means. Namaste is also not a word that belongs to any religion, as the people of that time believed that humanity is the only religion and that if we are not respecting the God in every human being and the natural ecosystem we live in, then, we are not respecting any God. Because God is not in any temple, church, mosque or ashram, but resides in each and every human being and we need to treat each and every human being with equal and same respect.

In late 2002, while getting ready to begin THE JOY OF GIVING movement, I was researching the Musahar community (*Musahar* means mice eaters and the community is called so because they survive by eating mice or grain they scrounge from the mouths of cattle since they live in a hopeless situation of abject chronic poverty), who are the so-called untouchables within the untouchables (Yes, within the untouchables also there is a hierarchy. We have reduced humanity to the lowest levels and made a laughing stock of ourselves). While going through the villages, in one village I had this elderly gentleman, who must have been all of five feet tall, pulling my kurta and pointing out to some mountains visible on the horizon. He then pulled me to his charpoy (a traditional light, low-cost woven bed used in the Indian subcontinent) and showed me a hammer and chisel and kept pointing to the mountains. I could not understand a word of what he was saying and struggled for over half hour to understand his mumblings. We then found another villager who spoke a little Hindi and explained to us that this is the honorable Dashrath Manjhi who cut the mountain with his bare hands and the hammer and chisel by working 10 hours every day of the week for 22 years. I first broke Mr. Manjhi's overwhelming story on **the Joy of Giving** website and then created www.iDishoom.com, the first portal to mainstream true stories of the real heroes who fight to RIGHT every WRONG.

For me, meeting Mr. Manjhi was a life-changing and mind-altering experience. It was Mr. Manjhi who inspired me to begin researching the heroic potential that each of us possesses and thus began my journey of discovering and telling stories of real heroes. Many of these heroes have now been awarded the Karmaveer Puraskaar and some have been featured in *Karma Kurry* Book 1 and this book. Mr. Manjhi inspired me to start the Karmaveer Puraskaar movement and was also chosen for the first Karmaveer Puraskaar. However, he died a few months prior to the first award ceremony, and even though he held no official position, was given a state funeral. Mr. Manjhi's story was made into a movie (*Manjhi*) by Ketan Mehta in 2015. We must remember that each one of us can unleash our potential with our small actions that would lead to the big change. To quote Confucius, "The human who moves mountains begins by carrying away small stones."

However, let me share with you about my research over the past 15 years from 2002, which inspired me to create the **moJOsh Inspirator** life and leadership lessons to INSPIRE SOLID CHARACTER and enable each and all of us to **unleash our heroic potential.** In 2009, while speaking at a conference on resilience- and strength-based strategies in

Croatia, I had another life-changing experience when I met the living legend Phil Zimbardo. **Philip George Zimbardo** is a psychologist and a professor emeritus at Stanford University. Popular for his 1971 Stanford Prison Experiment, he is also the founder and president of the Heroic Imagination Project, which was inspired by the Karmaveer movement.

With Phil's support, I embarked on path-breaking research through my leadership learning programs around the world and created the moJOsh Inspirator learning framework. The moJOsh Inspirator book based on **EVOLVED MINDFUL CONSCIOUSNESS** will be published later this year. Part of the learning has been shared in this book through simple ideas for action after each story to enable all our *Karma Kurry* readers to unleash their heroic potential.

moJOsh Inspirator is the human leadership path to discovering and unleashing your heroic potential. The book has compelling learning to awaken the hero in me and you. The learning consists of research from ancient and modern personal development literature, sciences, scientific and psychological experiments, case stories, neuroscience and human potential research of several ordinary heroes from around the world.

The moJOsh Inspirator learning consists of **3 magnificent mindsets, 7 valuable virtues and 21 priceless powers (values or principles)** that one can practice to inspire solid character and become a **moJOsh Inspirator by unleashing their unlimited potential.**

Friends, with my team members, my fellow learners, learning associates/partners, I undertook a 15-year qualitative research and in-depth study in developing the **moJOsh Inspirator mindsets and framework of virtues and powers**. For our learning **drafting and crafting** approach, we researched, interviewed, and **extensively observed over time** several participants (over 7,00,000 people and 1,80,000 + people directly) who I coached and worked with as a Consultant/Coach/Advisor/Mentor/Mentee. We then consolidated our findings into a series of patterns that helped us to understand the moJOsh Inspirator mindsets, beliefs, behaviors, virtues and powers.

So, friends, I wish you all the very best to unleash your heroic potential with the true stories of Real Heroes given in this book and *Karma Kurry* Book 1. When you read the stories, you will get insights, reflections and ideas for action to work on your own heroic potential. I wish you all a very happy journey of reading *Karma Kurry for the Hero in Me* and acting on the ideas to discover and develop your own heroic potential.

Happy reading!

Jai Hind

Jeroninio (Jerry) Almeida

P.S. We start the stories and moJOsh Inspirator learning with the number zero to understand the power of NOTHINGNESS or how the zero adds immense value to all other numbers and makes the vision bigger and better with planning and preparation to execute and act on the vision.

Jerry, who is inspired by real heroes like Mother Theresa, Bhagat Singh, Sukhdev, Rajguru, Chandrashekar Azad, Gandhi, Ikeda, King and Nelson Mandela, feels grateful that Karma Kurry got the last foreword ever written for a book from Mandela and has hence decided to never have any other foreword from anyone for the Karma Kurry book series. Book 1 of Karma Kurry was also launched in South Africa in 2016 with Ela Gandhi (Granddaughter of Mahatma Gandhi), along with other Mandela family members.

Seeking Answers

Anouradha Bakshi

Anouradha Bakshi's childhood was a privileged one; you could say she was born with a silver spoon in her mouth. Her father, Ram, was an Indian diplomat and her mother, Kamala, was a freedom fighter's daughter who steadfastly refused to be wed in British India. Her parents' love for India was profound and incomprehensible to Anou who grew up travelling around the world. She started speaking French before Hindi or English; she attended Mass with her Christian friends and fasted with her Muslim ones; she wore miniskirts, but she could also drape a sari whenever the need arose. To say that Anou and her parents were close would be an understatement; Anou's parents were godlike forces in her life and when they both passed away in quick succession, she was left an incomplete person.

She pined for a way to honour their memory and used her inheritance to set up a charitable trust bearing the name of her father, but was still without direction or peace of mind. In an act of desperation, Anou ventured to a part of Delhi previously unknown to her – a slum village lining the back of a university. Here, she met a healer and set out on a new path. The healer said, "Take your pain and make it into something your parents would be proud of." These simple words could have been easily dismissed, but Anou absorbed them and began looking for a sign.

The sign came in the form of a mentally and physically disabled young man named Manu. Manu lived – or rather roamed – the same street as the healer. He was half-clad, dirty and completely neglected. He was treated like an animal, fed with scraps and often pelted with stones by children, and when life became too much, he would break into deafening screams that went unheard. But Anou heard the screams and remembered the two lessons her father had taught her: the first, everything happens for a reason and, the second, that no life, however wretched, was without purpose. Manu's screams and her father's lessons reverberated through her mind and Anou acted on it with all her heart. She embraced Manu, something that had never been done and in that moment, she made a promise to herself that one day Manu would have a home, a warm bed, friends to laugh with and infinite love. Manu became the catalyst that would build Anou into a whole person again.

Now how to keep this promise became her problem. Anou had no social capital in that particular Delhi society, but first, she needed to win their trust before she could act on Manu's behalf. She remembered all the children who continually asked her to teach them to speak English and instinctively knew that spoken English classes would win the community's trust. The first person to step forward and offer help was Rani, the daughter of the healer. A high school dropout and only 15 at that time, Rani acted as Anou's guide, explaining the way the community worked. She was also one of the first people to sign up for the class. While children were taught in a rented jhuggi, Manu was bathed, fed, taken care of and provided with a safe place to sleep. At that moment, "Anou ma'am" was born and part of her promise to Manu was already fulfilled.

Anou speaks of Project Why's growth as an organic one: when a problem or a 'why' came her way, she would find the answer. Her inheritance appeared bountiful so when the spoken English students began asking for help with school work, it seemed that the only option was to set up a before-and-after school programme for primary school children. With this decision came a second one – to only use local men and women as teachers. The original Project Why's teachers had some education but were school dropouts due to early marriage or financial difficulties. These teachers were dedicated to Project Why and sensitive to the children's needs; however, the disadvantage was that their own English was poor. Project Why began utilizing foreign volunteers to assist the staff. Today, Project Why has 40 full-time teachers, found, trained and empowered from the slum communities; these teachers are further fortified by volunteers from all around the world.

'Whys' have continued to appear in front of Anou; when an older student arrived with cane welts he had received at school peppering his arm, Anou flew into a rage. She marched the student and his friends into the school and was met with teachers who could only be described as Dickensian; the teachers ridiculed the students and Anou for wanting to stick to a hopeless cause. Anou's outrage boiled over and she screamed, "These boys will pass their exams!" The very next day, a secondary class appeared

She threw herself into nearly daily blogs describing the gruesome plight of her students and their every miraculous achievement.

on the pavement across from the primary class. Yes, the boys passed their exams; yes, the secondary class still exists; yes, both boys and girls continue to pass their exams, often at the top of their class! And they are not caned.

Project Why's growth was destined to continue. Soon after the secondary programme began, a woman appeared with a gaggle of disabled children. The organization that previously supported these children had closed down without warning, leaving them destitute. The woman wanted to know if Project Why would step in. This was not only another 'why' for Anou but also a way to further fulfil her promise to Manu. These children could be his friends; he would have people to laugh with. Project Why's special section was opened with the help of Anou's daughter Shamika, who had trained with children with special needs. It seemed that the promise, at last, had been fulfilled, but this did not mean the end of Project Why. It was only the beginning.

As India evolved in haphazard ways to meet modern needs, Project Why adapted to suit new requirements; new programmes popped up continuously as the whys came into view – Heart Fix Hotel catered to children who needed open-heart surgery but could not afford it. This programme was actually spurred by an elderly man with a walking stick who had once come begging for money. His son needed an expensive open-heart surgery. Anou could not refuse and moved heaven and earth to pay for the surgery.

Anou also opened roadside classes for the Lohar gypsy children because she saw the need. Many would be discouraged by teaching on the road or in dumps, but Anou felt "anything would do as long as a child could learn."

It was no time at all before Anou's inheritance began to look dismally small and it dwindled faster every day. She fought the dilemma through fundraising, all by herself. "In hindsight," she says, "it was not the most intelligent thing to do as it would prove to be fragile and a hand-to-mouth model dependent on skills that I would not have been able to pass on." But for someone thinking and acting with her heart, it was an authentic choice. She threw herself into nearly daily blogs describing the gruesome plight of her students and their every miraculous achievement. Through her blogs, Anou told the story of India and finally saw the India her parents loved and described to her. A donor base was established and funds began to flow, freeing Anou to address other issues plaguing the society and focus on special projects.

One such project was Utpal. His family had moved into a shack next to the Project Why office when he was a baby. Every day, Anou would see the child and ask his parents when he would start in the crèche programme. One day the family disappeared and the neighbours said that Utpal had died. It was sad news but not a surprise. His mother had bipolar disorder and was an alcoholic; the fact that Utpal had survived until the age of one was extraordinary. However, Anou discovered that Utpal had not died; he had fallen into a pot of boiling water and been severely burned. The hospital released him, reporting his chance of survival as nil. But Anou looked into his beautiful eyes and whispered, "You and I have a long way to go." Utpal survived and has since come under the guardianship of Anou and Project Why. At the age of four, Utpal began attending a boarding school, a hard-won battle as the principal didn't believe a boy from the slums could compete with children from wealthy homes. Utpal proved them all wrong and his success led to seven other children joining him at the boarding school, including another burn victim. Today, Utpal is a teenager and thriving at the boarding school; he is at the top of his class as are the other seven kids.

Utpal and his journey brought two other social issues to the forefront for Project Why: life skills for distressed women and children. Utpal's mother not only suffered from bipolar disorder and alcoholism but also from a lack of marketable skills. This inspired the Women's Centre, which offers English language, beautician and sewing classes to slum women, ensuring that they have a source of income if needed. The Women's Centre also offers primary and secondary classes because the women couldn't leave their children alone while they attended their own classes. Before Utpal and his cohorts entered the boarding school, it was apparent that they wouldn't fit in because they didn't have the same social skill set as that of the middle-class children. A residential programme was established to teach essential skills, like eating with a fork and knife.

Anou's story seems like a myriad of happy accidents that resulted in Project Why, but the truth is that she had to fight every single step of the way. As Project Why expanded, she had to gain the trust of new communities and many distrusted her motives. The staff would arrive in the mornings to find their schools destroyed, forcing the classes to take place on the road, under a bridge or in a dump. However, Project Why persevered. Anou received death threats and met them head-on, confronting the community, which backed down as soon as Project Why produced results. Funding continued to pose a problem as Project Why couldn't accept money from the government without becoming a mere puppet under bureaucratic control. Anou made foreign contacts who set up their own organizations to help fund her work; she had found others who, too, saw with their hearts.

Anou's greatest feat has not been the creation of Project Why; it's actually her ability to see with her heart. Project Why is just one manifestation of Anou seeing the world with her heart first and her eyes second.

Today, Project Why runs smoothly with two directors under Anou – Rani and Dharmendra. Rani, since the beginning of Project Why, has passed her class X and XII boards, graduated from college and has become fluent in English. Anou often jokes that her directors are so effective in their roles that she has become redundant. There are over 900 students in their classes altogether. There are three main locations for the classes so that a greater number of children can be reached. Anou no longer spends her days teaching English or making funny faces with the crèche students; she has put herself to work full-time marketing Project Why. Her blogs continue to appear almost daily. She has published one book, *Dear Popples,* and is working on a second, while at the same time connecting with potential donors and volunteers.

This is how I came to meet Anou: I arrived at Project Why as a volunteer, fresh from high school and landed on her couch one day for a meeting along with several other volunteers. The word 'charismatic' does not do Anou justice; I was mesmerized by her presence and listened in silence to story after story about Project Why. I felt an immediate and intense surge of love, for Project Why, for India, for Anou, and I stayed for six months, living with Anou and her family. I now return yearly because Anou's family and Project Why have become my own family. I know I am not the only one Anou has had this effect on. Just as everything Midas touched turned to gold, everyone Anou touches begins to see with his or her heart.

As always, the future of Project Why is a precarious one as funding waxes and wanes. Anou is hoping to leave the running of Project Why to her directors and her daughter very soon, but before that, she is planning to initiate a new programme (or two!). A new and sustainable location will be developed to house a skills lab. Beyond basic education, the students at Project Why need skills they can use to go into the world and make a living. All students have different abilities and limitations, so Anou plans to offer an array of skills, including foreign languages, computer programming, dance, art, culinary arts, etc. Trained professionals and volunteers would fill in the gaps in the local teachers' knowledge. For instance, it recently came to the attention of Project Why that an elderly man has been educating some village children on the outskirts of Delhi; he has been doing so in his own time and with his own money. Anou hopes to assimilate his programme into Project Why, providing his class with school supplies, a midday meal and the potential for expansion as well as compensation for his efforts.

Anou's greatest feat has not been the creation of Project Why; it's actually her ability to see with her heart. Project Why is just one manifestation of Anou seeing the world with her heart first and her eyes second. She goes through the world not seeing the way everyone else does, but feeling far more than most do. She has never allowed her naiveté to halt her in the quest to answer the whys and has no plans to stop either. Despite all her accomplishments and planned ventures, Anou still believes she has yet to sing her swan song.

Biographer

Emily Fox is a student at Bard College in Annandale-on-Hudson, New York, studying religion. She first visited Project Why at 18 and fell in love with India, and she returns at least once a year. Emily is currently working on creating a US-based NGO to support Project Why and expand the donor base and volunteer pool. Until then, Emily continues to help Project Why from USA and pine after *baingan bharta* and *khandvi*.

moJOsh Inspirator Power 0:
The Power of Vision and Execution

"Each night, when I go to sleep, I die. And the next morning, when I wake up, I am reborn."

~ Mahatma Gandhi

Thought Leadership for Reflection: Most people do not like to think of death, without realizing that the race towards death begins the day we are born. It is good to think of our death as it helps us to know that we have limited time and that we should therefore BE ALIVE and THRIVE in every moment of our life. Who knows what would happen in the next moment. And thus, thinking of our death enables us to USE TIME WISELY to make meaningful contributions in every moment of our life. It also helps us to envision the legacy we want to create in our lifetime and execute the same with excellence. After all, we know we will die one day and if we are alive, we can find a way to execute and act on our vision with integrity by using every moment of life well.

Ideas for Action: In life, we all get broken at some time or the other. When broken, most give up and BreakDown, some have a plan and are prepared to persevere and BreakThrough. That is what defines the champions of change, who unleash that miracle within. These are real heroes who START THEIR LIFE with the end in mind and while they struggle to achieve the end, they never forget to ENJOY and LIVE the journey. It may seem paradoxical, but talking about death can give us an immediate and renewed vitality. In fact, in 2013, two academic researchers (Christopher R. Long and Dara N. Greenwood) found that talking about death actually makes us funnier. Thinking about our death helps us to enjoy each morning when we wake up and be grateful each night when we got to sleep with the hope of waking up the next day.

1

Making a Change with Dot-com

Anupam Mittal

Eight years ago, I received this rare opportunity to work for a young, dynamic businessman like Anupam Mittal, who is known for his memorable personality. I say memorable because there's a lot of insight into his personality; highly professional and yet also openly human. He gets excited when things go well, appreciates hard work, and when thing go wrong, he gets disappointed, not in others, but in himself.

He has always showed up where it matters the most, in the minds and hearts of his people. He is a people's person. As a matter of fact, there are a lot of people at higher ranks in a hierarchy who would show concern to a minor when he or she is going through a rough patch in life or is suffering from some crisis. But, the way Anupam deals with this is a little different: by *being* concerned about them.

I always follow the first lesson Anupam taught me: learn to add value to what you do. In the beginning, I was not able to understand it. I very well knew it as 'value addition', but was never able to actually put it into action. Understanding his objective was the most important goal for me. I had to familiarize myself with doing things in a particular way. Slowly and steadily, I started learning what he was looking for in the role that I was playing.

Anupam is very much determined to get his message across in its true essence. He chooses his words very carefully to create an impact on the listener. Because belief is what shapes a personality, and the personality of the employees, in turn, shapes the image of the company.

Among Anupam's businesses is the now-famous Shaadi. com with the accomplishment of bringing over three million people together and the distinction of becoming one of India's most valuable Internet companies. He has also founded businesses such as Makaan.com to make the process of finding homes more efficient and Mauj Mobile which runs one of the world's largest app stores called Mobango. Anupam is also an active angel investor and has seed-funded several entrepreneurs who have gone on to build significant enterprises in their own right.

Anupam was exposed to business from a very early age; his father is a successful businessman who had gone from earning ₹150 in monthly salary to building a textile business comprising three medium-sized factories manufacturing over two million metres of cotton fabric every month. His mother is a housewife but also dedicates considerable time towards the upliftment of tribal people in India. He has two sisters, who have set up their own fashion and wedding-planning businesses over the years.

While growing up, Anupam was a very shy and reserved child, but a fairly good student. He possessed a rather curious intellect from his early years and often asked questions to his parents and people around him, which besides being difficult to answer, were rather rare for someone his age. He constantly questioned the status quo and at the age of 13, took up his first significant project. When he noticed that there was no sports club in his housing society, Anupam got a few of his friends together and took it upon himself to have one built. The group challenged the managing committee and against all odds, was successful in getting their commitment on building a sports club in the society. They developed the club and it went on to last for 20 years, providing young people a place to productively expend their energy and time. Anupam would realize much later in life that this experience gave him the confidence to affect change.

During college, Anupam was not very impressed with the

prevailing system of education and learnt more outside the classroom than inside. His restlessness led him to join his father's business, but within a couple of years, elt he wasn't contributing much, nor was he really 'making a difference'. He yelled "plot twist" and moved on. As a result, he dabbled in a few different projects and ultimately started his own business of exporting cotton made-ups to Europe. He was able to bag orders, set up factories, enter into outsourcing contracts, and eventually build capacity to manufacture over five million cotton bags per month. As luck would have it, cotton prices shot up and Anupam could not sustain his business. "None of it tastes like cotton candy," he said, giving a wicked grin! While he could have walked away from honouring his contract, I remember him saying, "I would rather be bankrupt than go back on my word." He had to shut shop amidst losses. He decided he had much to learn.

A serendipitous meeting with a matchmaker got him wondering about the limited opportunities Indians have to find potential life partners and so he decided to right this wrong by using the Internet.

As a result, Anupam spent the following year travelling through Europe and the US, doing odd jobs and observing life upfront. He was struck by the sense of justice, equality and fairness in the West. He was particularly impressed by the work ethic and sincerity that he observed in the US and felt that he could draw from living in that environment. Anupam enrolled into an MBA programme in Boston and prepared himself for the most defining period of his life. From the very first day, Anupam took to the 'American way' instantly. He thrived in the merit-based system, where hard work, sincerity and integrity were rewarded. He was pleasantly surprised when his professors encouraged students to disagree with them, unlike the authoritarian systems in India. The most memorable days ended with the dirtiest clothes. Doing his own laundry, cooking his own food, making friends from different cultures, being exposed to countless ideas, was all very therapeutic for him. He came into his own, realized the value of his opinions and ideas, and the potential that any individual can have. He found strength and wisdom in exploring one's own path in life.

In 1998, Anupam visited India for a few months and was surprised by the opportunities he saw all around. Having been away for a couple of years, he was able to see things dispassionately and objectively. He felt it would be a good time to experiment setting up a business and so he founded SatyaNet Solutions as an experiment, hiring a few designers and programmers.

Anupam is very much determined to get his message across in its true essence. He chooses his words very carefully to create an impact on the listener.

A serendipitous meeting with a matchmaker got him wondering about the limited opportunities that Indians have to find potential life partners and so he decided to right this wrong by using the Internet to find a life partner and therefore taking away geographical and spatial limitations. He charted out the first matchmaking website in the world, directed his team to develop the site and returned to his IT consulting job in the US.

Back in the US, the Internet was booming and Anupam's company diversified into the platform. He quickly rose to senior management with a significant span of responsibility. He spent evenings and weekends working with his team in India to launch Shaadi.com. But it was not an instant hit. While he continued to work with his team to evolve the business model in India, the dot-com boom was firmly in place in the US. By the time he was 28, he had become a millionaire by way of his stock options from his job in the US. By then, Anupam had learnt how to manage and develop teams and businesses, but harder lessons were still in store.

By 2000, the Internet as an industry imploded and so did Anupam's financial situation. He went from being a millionaire to penniless overnight. He could no longer finance his operations in India and started to think about becoming a full-time entrepreneur. He observed that Shaadi. com was showing the potential of someday becoming a large business with the changing aspirations of the Indian youth. He quit his job and returned to India with the sole purpose of creating an entrepreneurial success story out of Shaadi.com.

Anupam's job was cut out for him. Not only did he find it challenging to attract people to a fledgling company run by an unknown entrepreneur, he found his idea being ridiculed and not being taken seriously. His determination and 'can do' attitude egged him on. He would often say, "One day, they will understand."

By 2004, Shaadi.com had become a household name through sheer perseverance, smart marketing and its first-mover advantage. Anupam used his lead to launch other businesses such as Makaan.com and Mauj Mobile, which have gone on to help redefine emerging industries such as online media, digital music and content.

In 2006, Anupam started to realize that there were many like him who questioned the status quo and dreamt of creating new enterprises. While a few had access to the resources and personal networks to enable them to do so, the majority were handicapped due to the lack of early-stage funding and mentorship available in India. He developed a passion for entrepreneurship and early-stage funding, and started to seed and mentor companies with strong founding teams and credible ideas. Often he funded business plans that were scribbled on a piece of paper. Some of the companies went on to raise venture capital and private equity capital and Anupam started being recognized as a leading entrepreneur, winning several Indian and global awards and recognition. He also found a mention in lists such as the *Business Week*'s 50 Most Powerful People in India. His companies started to be recognized as path-breaking and were counted amongst some of the world's most innovative companies alongside names such as Apple, Google and Facebook. His brands Shaadi.com and Makaan.com have now become household names.

Over the last couple of years, Anupam has started to direct some of his energy and resources towards affecting positive change in society. He is attempting to do this through the simple philosophy that for corporate houses to bring about significant and sustainable change, their efforts must be aligned with their businesses in the direction of fulfilling it. Not only does this keep the activities focused and measurable, it creates a virtuous cycle for both business and society.

As a result of this belief, he and his companies have identified three areas towards which they are directing their efforts to in the immediate term. Shaadi.com is addressing the wrong of dowry, while Makaan.com will focus on affecting change in government policies to make housing a fundamental right for every citizen. Mauj Mobile will direct resources towards sustainable recycling of mobile phones, an increasing menace for the environment.

Shaadi.com's anti-dowry campaign began with the launch of the game called 'Angry Brides' where a player throws weapons such as shoes, utensils and other household items on grooms demanding dowry. Every hit leads to a contribution to the anti-dowry fund. The game went viral within its first week and saw over five lakh downloads, was exposed to over five million people on Facebook and was covered by global media such as *CNN*, *BBC*, *The Wall Street Journal*, *Forbes* and the like, reaching over 100 million people across the globe.

The year 2014 witnessed a revolution called #FastForHer, a social initiative set out to take a stand and promote equality in marriage through the occasion of *Karwa Chauth*. The idea of #FastForHer went viral when Anupam took the pledge on Twitter and nominated author Chetan Bhagat and others to follow suit.

Makaan.com has begun its housing initiatives by launching the property intelligence portal called MakaanIQ. The team behind MakaanIQ is attempting to organize real estate-related information and intelligence in India, which so far has been hard to come by. The more organized the information, the more transparent the industry, and that, in turn, will create an opportunity for change.

Anupam also dreams of restarting his film division called People Pictures, which produced *Flavors* and *99*, and making films that can affect social change. His vision for entrepreneurship in India is that it ultimately becomes global in nature. He is working towards that goal through angel investing and helping put a roadmap in place for infrastructure required for entrepreneurship to flourish. He feels that the new crop of entrepreneurs in India should focus on global ideas and markets as opposed to simply providing services to the west.

According to him, India has played the arbitrage angle for too long and it is time we thought of ourselves as creators, inventors and innovators. He hopes that the next Facebook or Google will come out of India, raising aspirations of a billion people. Until then, he wants to keep his head down and continue his relentless pursuit of making a difference in the world.

Anupam believes in the adage 'Be brave and be good, and heavenly forces will come to your aid.'

Biographer

Mary Lobo is an associate of Anupam Mittal and an ardent salsa dancer who hails from the city of dreams, Mumbai.

moJOsh Inspirator Power 1:
The Power of Integrity

"Integrity is doing the right thing, even when no one is watching."

~ C.S. Lewis

Thought Leadership for Reflection: Integrity is doing what you say by understanding what is right. Integrity is not the reputation we display; it is the character we live, even in times of adversity and hardship. Integrity is doing the right thing even when it's much easier not to. Integrity is about being true to yourself and the guiding principles of humanity.

Ideas for Action: Self-discovery and awareness, social consciousness, human values, conscience and moral intelligence help one to develop integrity. This is turn helps one to be true to the self and to pursue passion and goals with élan and peace of mind. Remember, wrong is wrong even if everyone is doing it and integrity is walking the path less trodden even when no one is going that way.

2

Devotion from a Bird's-eye View

Aseem Asha Usman

How would I have known that my heart would discover a blessed nest in New Delhi as I trod upon New York City's teeming pavements? Much more than an ocean separates these streets from that paradoxical place of ancient spirituality, Bollywood extravaganza and crushing poverty.

In my metropolis along the Hudson, the 'reality show' fame is hungrily sought, achieved and snatched away at the blink of an eye. The average worker earns more than enough to afford the luxury of a daily latte – "with soy milk and a double shot of espresso, if you please!" And the most common experience of worship takes place in SoHo boutiques.

To be fair, pocketed here and there throughout the city are not only many good-hearted individuals, but genuine places of spiritual respite, such as churches, synagogues, temples, meditation centres of all kinds, and even a mosque or two. Yet sadly, and unlike what classic comic books might have us believe, there is certainly a paucity of superheroes in this Gotham. Where are those shining lights capable of dazzling us with their extraordinary feats of self-sacrifice for the betterment of mankind? How misguided I was in the past to assume such champions are garbed only in colourful Spandex and glittering helmets.

About a year ago, I received a friend request from an unknown individual via a popular social network website. His name was Aseem Asha Usman, from New Delhi. I accepted.

For several years prior, an attraction to the faraway land of India had been growing steadily within me. This was especially so for its deep association with mysticism, an inner realm of lifelong appeal. Gratefully, I had stumbled upon the work of the late Eknath Easwaran. This renowned spiritual teacher was born in Kerala before relocating to the United States, where he helped introduce several generations to the tremendous benefits of meditation. Through Easwaran's profoundly rich translations of *The Upanishads*, *The Dhammapada* and *The Bhagavad Gita*, the glories of Indian spirituality opened a sacred space within me. It seemed the Roman Catholic saviour of my Western upbringing was joining hands with that of a most beloved blue divinity who happens to be a supreme flautist.

Eventually, I encountered the joyously challenging work of the Sufi mystics. Perhaps it was by their inclusion among my favourite books posted at the said social network which drew Aseem to make contact initially, for we both share a mutual passion for their all-embracing perspective celebrating the message of love, harmony and beauty underlying all religions – the divine spark shared by all.

In very short order, Aseem and I began a vibrant dialogue. Through it, I learned of his credentials – quite impressive for someone only in their early 30s. Aseem is a science graduate from the Aligarh Muslim University. In 2005, he completed his PG Diploma in development communication at AJK Mass Communication Research Centre of Jamia Millia Islamia, New Delhi. In addition, he has been mentored by eminent film director Muzaffar Ali, renowned fine artist Jatin Das and Oscar-winning composer A. R. Rahman.

With my own background in film, I was intrigued to learn of one of Aseem's primary activities – to spread awareness on local issues by making short documentary films and through a variety of other digital media and visual art forms. A trained filmmaker, Aseem has taught hundreds the innovative use of new media tools and technologies at his centres in Jafrabad-Seelampur and Okhla Village. In addition to filmmaking and photography, courses on English, computer sciences and relating to the internet are also made available. All of this is supplemented by attending lectures and interacting with an impressive roster of luminary guests such as filmmaker Benoy K. Behl, musicians Fateh and Murad Ali, dancer and choreographer Astad Deboo, actor and activist Rahul Bose, writer and media activist Dr. Partha Banerjee, actress Rohini Hattangadi, dancer Manjari Chaturvedi, documentary filmmaker Himanshu Malhotra, photographer Raghu Rai and film editor Sabina Kidwai, among others. There are also regular visits to a wide variety of arts organizations balanced with attendance at innumerable sacred ceremonies and celebrations.

The majority of the students are women and children from various marginalized and mainstream communities. Their short documentaries and digital print designs have come to serve as a powerful voice speaking on timely and often socially-denied issues impacting women and children. These have included eve-teasing, discrimination against the girl child, human trafficking, slavery, female foeticide, women's education and the rights and the role of Islamic women in the modern Muslim world.

How misguided I was in the past to assume that champions are garbed only in colorful Spandex and glittering helmets.

The films have been disseminated on local, state, national and international levels through a variety of platforms. In this way, Aseem's grass-root efforts have promoted global peace and brotherhood. Here, he explains the genesis of this dedicated vocation:

"I believe one of the deciding moments of my life happened when I chose not to pursue a career in mainstream media, neither at a major television network nor at a commercial film studio. I still remember how during his visits to my college, the eminent film director Shyam Benegal repeatedly asked us *not* to use film and media for 'glare'. Instead, he urged us to direct our efforts toward the most marginalized and neediest of people – to reveal the real problems of their everyday existence.

"This message changed the course of my life and dissolved any appeal Bollywood and the daily television soaps might have held over me. Instead, I became determined to undertake something more meaningful. After finishing my degree at AJK Mass Communication College, my teacher sent me to a grass-roots non-governmental organization which was working with UNESCO in east Delhi's slum areas. The seed-funding for my projects was provided by the local people who did not want me to leave. They offered me space in a local jeans factory. My former students mobilized their friends and relatives to join my courses in design and visual communication. Many of them had already learned media skills from me. They paid me fees to sustain the project. Space, electricity and maintenance were provided free of cost. The eminent composer, A. R. Rahman, provided for the installing of computers and that is how I started working without a budget. At one time, I also provided free home tutorials to the owner's children in return for utilizing the space.

"Throughout my life, I encountered many women who had been victims of domestic violence. Some of my young friends during my school days used to talk about their mothers and household problems. These painful stories always remained in my heart. So I started publishing a Hindi newsletter with the women from the slums of East Delhi focusing on their issues. This monthly paper was appreciated widely. Slowly, I began to offer training in journalistic reporting to local women – the very same women who circulated more than 2,000 copies of the paper door to door each month."

Soon, UNESCO and Queensland University of Technology (QUT), Australia, took notice. As an outgrowth of the newsletter project, those organizations proposed Aseem to expand his mode of expression to a digital film format. The subject would continue to be the plight of repressed women from the Seelampur slums of New Delhi. Prior to this, Aseem had already met and recorded the brutal experiences of thousands of this downtrodden population as part of an ethnographic research for the 'Finding a Voice' project on empowering marginalized communities through digital literacy.

He says, "How could I remain blind to what had to be done to expose their [women's] issues? I must add how there were several political and religious groups strongly resistant against such filmmaking at that time. In fact, I was threatened personally far more than once. You see, there was an objection to any filmmaking at all by women. First, because photography is not allowed according to the stricter rules of Islam; and second, women's activities are typically limited to taking care of the family within the confines of the home. Furthermore, no woman should be working with a man – especially an unknown commodity as me!

"But somehow, I was able to begin a dialogue with those who had initially attempted to defeat the project. In time, they converted into some of our greatest supporters. In the end, many schools, non-profit organizations and individuals collaborated with me and championed the programme's survival."

As the subject of many of the films produced, Aseem's efforts spotlighted perhaps the most defenseless portion of this maltreated sector often disregarded entirely: "I found children were the indirect victims of domestic violence. Fortunately, our contact inspired them to raise their innocent voices against such abuse. They, too, joined our cause. Together, we made short digital stories and screened them in their communities. One of the key topics was gender-based violence and its impact on children. The community people, especially men, attended the screenings which resulted in a lot of discussion. Fortunately, many men stopped the cycle of maltreatment and joined our campaign to sensitize others on this issue. Gradually, it became an authentic movement, with many local non-governmental organizations and schools joining us as well."

The natural next step was to formally develop Flying Birds of India. The group was established in early 2005 at AJK Mass Communication Research Centre. Later, that same year, children affected by the Gujarat riots joined it and produced some print designs based on poetry by the Sufi poets Khusrau and Rumi. Then in 2006, the young women of urban slums of Delhi joined the group. Flying Birds began to produce films through Community Media Initiative (CMI) to screen them in different areas in order to raise consciousness on the urgent issues represented therein.

"How could I remain blind to what had to be done to expose their [women's] issues?"

~ Aseem Asha Usman

As for the films, the consistent quality of what these young people, newly educated in the art form of filmmaking are making on an almost daily basis, is remarkable. With less than shoestring budgets and the most basic equipment, under Aseem's expert eye they are able to delve into the heart of the topic at hand with a directness that never ceases to astonish. Here is a rare example of art functioning as a catalyst toward social change.

One of Aseem's most transformative programmes is the *Udaan* Community Film Festival. Inaugurated in 2006, this ongoing series is a convergence of art and cinema for social change. The programme's aim is to bring younger minds in contact with their communities and heritage by providing support for the creative expression of their hopes, ideas, feelings and imaginations. These are reflected in the short documentary films made by Flying Birds of India and screened at the one-day film festival organized in collaboration with other non-profit organizations and academic institutions from within or outside the community.

If there's one person whom Aseem never fails to offer his gratitude, it is A. R. Rahman. With characteristic benevolence, the renowned composer has made several key programmes possible by donating computers and even his own personal Handycam. In appreciation of Aseem's efforts, A. R. Rahman has written:

"I have been witness to the noble work Aseem Asha Foundation is engaged in. They provide providing courses in performing arts, film and digital audio-visual media techniques to disadvantaged communities especially women and girl children, which has over the years helped individuals in pursuing careers in media. Aseem's other initiatives, The Flying Birds of India and *Udaan* community film festival, are also noteworthy."

Director and screenwriter Shyam Benegal has also provided much-needed support. As Aseem describes him thusly: "Shyam Benegal has been a very encouraging soul. I was deeply inspired by his film *Manthan,* in which a milk co-operative society was formed with the participation of the villagers. Seeing his other films, such as *Zubedia,* developed my understanding of Muslim gender issues. I have continued to send Shyam updates about my work and he has called me many times with encouraging words."

The person with whom the heartbeat of Aseem's work begins is his very first guru – his beloved mother. While speaking of his mother, Aseem says, "I was an extremely determined kid. Raised in a very open family, I was constantly exposed to the myriad cultures, traditions and customs of India. So early on, I learned a lot within this pluralistic atmosphere. Importantly, too, my mother is a supportive critic of my work. Since childhood, she enlightened me through wise advice and realistic goal-setting. She has been the only one who bore all the pressures both in and outside the home, never pushing me to work for monetary reasons alone. She understood and fostered my early awareness of social injustice. For these reasons, my mother's surname is attached to my name before my father's, to recognize my eternal respect for her innumerable sacrifices on my behalf.

My overseeing organization, Aseem Asha Foundation is humbly dedicated to her many sacrifices which have allowed my spirit to follow an uncommon and worthwhile path."

Without question, Aseem's efforts are more than admirable. Yet speaking practically, what would be their ultimate worth if there were no observable results to speak of? Happily, in less than half a decade, the success stories are countless. There is Kalam who works in television production for a local channel; Kehkashan, a computer trainer; Nazreen, a graphic designer; and Iqra, a marketing executive for a Dubai-based cosmetics company. Others soaring from the flock have found valued employment as hospital nurses, bank workers, retail salespersons, administrators, sports trainers, and teachers of all kinds.

Mushtaq and Kiran are particularly outstanding success stories. Aseem speaks of his protégés with the understandable pride of a new parent: "Mushtaq belongs to a poor family. His father is a gardener; his mother a housemaid; and. his brothers work as electricians, tailors and labourers. Mushtaq lives in a room of less than ten square feet in size. His career options were limited within that sphere before joining one of our centres. Since then, Mushtaq has not only improved his academics but also learned the technical and conceptual aspects of filmmaking through my workshops. As a result, he has produced several outstanding films for our community film festivals. His short [story] on Tagore was recently released via the Tony Blair Faith Foundation website. Mushtaq has a concrete career before him. Earlier, he used to study in Urdu at a government school. Now, he attends an English-medium school where he (recently) ranked as the third top student in his class. With typical kindness, A.R. Rahman graciously donated for his tuition. Mushtaq has become a source of inspiration in his community. To date, he has brought more than 50 children and women to the centre."

In the same way, Kiran from Seelampur has been employed as a programme coordinator in several non-profit agencies following her training from Aseem's centre. This allows her to support her family. Kiran still volunteers with Flying Birds. And just this year, she has been admitted to a course in mass communication. I am happy to report how a kind donor had provided financial aid for her tuition.

A common tragedy among those from dire origins is a sense of hopelessness. Sadly, such a seriously damaging emotional state is all too often a simply realistic response to overwhelming difficulties. For is it not accurate how all too many 'civilized' societies are designed carefully to protect those in power, at the severe detriment of others? For the unfortunate in this cruel equation, a sense of self-defeating malaise seems unavoidable. For many, it is perhaps easier to abandon any sense of optimism and effort for a potentially brighter outcome. Almost every spiritual tradition points towards a similar catalyst to shift such inequity – and that is the tremendous power of selfless love and compassion. And these are the twin core motivators fueling Aseem's day-to-day activities. Surely, this gives evidence of a heart being capable of moving mountains and removing seemingly insurmountable obstacles.

In his leadership, Aseem demonstrates humility, continually refreshed from a deeply spiritual and selfless source.

Within the great majority of those passing through Aseem's programmes, a newfound reality is born – one fostering self-worth and courage. Undoubtedly, this is all engendered by viable skills resulting in horizons brighter than ever thought possible. Happily, upcoming generations of Flying Birds should be heading towards extremely positive prospects. Aseem's indefatigable striving to bring about awareness to the tragic state of India's disenfranchised through the media has received real success. One only hopes that much-needed financial support is not far behind.

Amazingly to date, no funding agency is supporting Aseem's many programmes. He is currently in the midst of completing the complex, required documentation for his educational trust. In Aseem's words: "My Facebook friends have always helped me to expand my ideas and whenever funds are required, they are of help. One friend who lives in the United States organized a concert/photo exhibition to benefit The Flying Birds of India. With the help of many individuals, I have expanded my programmes. I have also raised funds by providing Mixed Media Storytelling Workshops for national NGOs and individuals. Mushtaq and I have also produced commercials with the Flying Birds team to raise money for the projects. We have expanded our coaching programmes, where academic and competitive coaching is provided. These students pay tuition, which helps us to run the foundation's other programmes."

Still, he finds contentment in serving his community by combining his two great passions – social work and the arts. Aseem pinpoints the fruitful harvest of his work thus far: "There has been a great impact on the parents of the women and children associated with my projects in the slums of Okhla and Seelampur. The residents there are now more receptive to allowing their girls' real careers outside the home. More than 25 women students from our Seelampur centre are working in the mainstream market and earning decent wages. I am so pleased to see them develop the art of inspiring others to join us, too! We have never even published a single pamphlet publicizing our work. Word of mouth alone has helped to mobilize our efforts. Those leaving our programmes as well as their families have been sending new candidates to learn from our centres."

Aseem is very clear about what his plans are for the future. He urges the youth to voice their opinions about the issues that bother them, instead of wasting time and energy on negative attractions. According to Aseem, the young must take the time to understand various cultures of the world, to weave a singular vision for the development of a unified global consciousness free of injustice. After doing this, they should use their talents to serve their countries. He says, "Our hope is to open many media training centres throughout India and the world, and to organize national and international community film festivals in various cities and villages of India and the world. In this way, a healthy exchange of ideas can take place, and communities can grow and help evolve the traditional mindset. I would like to reach many more unaided women of the world who are still speechless and suffering from severe gender-based violence."

On a personal note, as a typical Westerner, I must claim my previous ignorance as to the great difficulties these young communities face on so many levels regularly. Through my small involvement, I have received an amazing education not only of the mind, but surely and more importantly, of the heart. Aseem and Flying Birds are truly rays of hope in this world.

Simple words cannot convey how deeply impressed I am with Aseem's tireless undertakings. In his leadership, Aseem demonstrates humility continually refreshed from a deeply spiritual and selfless source. He touches upon the horizons he has expanded for so many.

Biographer

Michael Orlando Yaccarino gained recognition for his analyses of genre films and interviews with their makers. His writings on fashion, music and unconventional historical figures, as well as poetry, have appeared worldwide. With Scot D. Ryersson, he is the co-director of The Casati Archives and co-author of the international bestselling biographies *Infinite Variety: The Life and Legend of the Marchesa Casati* and *The Marchesa Casati: Portraits of a Muse*; the play *Infinite Variety: Portrait of a Muse*; as well as the critically-acclaimed fairy tale *The Princess of Wax*. He is a student of the tanpura and the Sufi path. Based in the

United States, Michael is an international member of the Advisory Committee for Flying Birds of India and Aseem Asha Foundation.

moJOsh Inspirator Power 2:
The Power of Dignity

"The greatest difficulty is that men do not think enough of themselves, do not consider what it is that they are sacrificing when they follow in a herd, or when they cater for their establishment."

~ Ralph Waldo Emerson

Thought Leadership for Reflection: To live a simple life of honour, righteousness and respect is the greatest achievement in a lifetime. If we have dignity, we will never partner with any wrongdoer or partake in any wrongdoing that would reduce or hurt our self-respect. Remember: Respect starts with me and I would never do anything wrong that harms my dignity and the ability to walk with my head held high.

Ideas for Action: Learn how to respect oneself and be whole as a person and a human being. Your integrity to create respect for yourself and your near and dear ones will always help you to stay on the right path even in the most trying and tempting times. In today's world, remember wrong is wrong even if most are doing it, but right is right even though very few are doing it.

3

Vitamin C3 for the Tribals: Cure, Care & Compassion

Dr. Ashish Satav

"Let him die," said the tribal widow with resignation, as Dr. Ashish Satav tried persuading her to admit her two-year-old son to his hospital. The child, on top of being severely malnourished, was suffering from pneumonia and in a serious condition. The good doctor observed that the little boy's chest was studded with rice, red liquid and feathers of hen; his skin had burn marks and there was a garland of garlic hanging around his neck – clearly the items given by a traditional faith healer. These were superstitious practices followed by the tribal people to cure diseases. Going to the doctor was the last resort. Ashish relentlessly pleaded with the mother to admit her son to the hospital and stay with him, else the boy would die at home. That's when the mother made the above remark with a fatalistic sadness and added, "At home, I have four more children, goats and chicken to look after and anyway he is going to die!" She went back to her village with the child and three days later Ashish got the message that the boy had died.

This incident took place in one of the poorest and most deprived parts of India – Melghat in Maharashtra, where mortality rates among children under five years of age were twice that of the national average. Melghat was known in those days for just two things: malnutrition and Project Tiger, a wildlife conservation project launched in 1972 by the then Prime Minister Indira Gandhi to protect the diminishing population of Indian tigers. A few years ago, Ashish had started one of the first hospitals in this region, consisting of a hut and four rooms, in a rented house. The house served as the Out Patient Department (OPD), had a couple of rooms for indoor patients, and doubled up as his residence.

Young Ashish grew up in Wardha and his grandfather Shri Vasantrao Bombatkar, a Sarvodaya Movement leader, greatly influenced the shaping of his thoughts and beliefs, especially through the books of Mahatma Gandhi, Swami Vivekananda and Vinoba Bhave. Gandhiji's clarion call for youths to go back to the villages for village reconstruction and to serve rural India (for the real India lives in her villages) made Ashish decide to study medicine and work in the rural parts of India.

Since there was no cook in the hospital, Kavita herself would prepare meals for her patients and feed them.

While pursuing his MBBS and later his MD at Government Medical College, Nagpur, he visited tribal health projects run by Drs. Prakash and Manda Amte and Drs. Abhay and Rani Bang, Dr. Ravindra Kolhe and Dr. Sudarshan. He realized that tribal areas needed medical facilities to a much larger extent, and especially found Melghat to be the neediest region with insufficient health facilities.

To acclimatize himself to the rigors of practicing medicine in poor rural environments, Ashish followed a simple lifestyle. During the scorching summers of Nagpur, where temperatures hovered around 45 degrees, he would stay in his room without a cooler or fan, and during winters where temperatures plunged to 10 degrees, he would take bath with cold water. With regular yoga and meditation, he gradually learnt to control inherent desires like greed, egoistic attitude, sexual desires, envy and anger. All these practices gave him the mental capacity and physical stamina to work with equanimity in the face of future ordeals.

Ashish's goal to serve rural communities started as a spark and soon blazed into a glowing flame when in 1998 he resigned from the post of lecturer at Mahatma

Gandhi Institute of Medical Sciences, Sevagram, and registered a voluntary organization, MAHAN (an acronym for **M**-Meditation, **A**-AIDS, **H**-Health, **A**-De-**A**ddiction, **N**-Nutrition). With his own savings of around ₹1, lakh he started a small hospital in Dharni, Melghat. At first, there was no financial support from anyone, but a few months later, Dr. Sushila Nayar from Kasturba Health Society (KHS), provided funds to the hospital. Since then, MAHAN has been running in partnership with KHS.

The first couple of years of running the hospital were an endless struggle. Due to a lack of trained staff, Ashish initially managed everything single-handedly with the help of a 9th pass youth. Those days there would hardly be three or four patients visiting the OPD each day. The tribal people did not have much faith in doctors and suspected whether a doctor living in a hut and using a bicycle was really a qualified one. Therefore, Ashish went to the villages himself to raise health awareness amongst the tribal people. However, travelling to the villages from Dharni was no mean task. One had to travel at least 50 km; the roads passed through mountains and dense forests with wild animals. During the monsoons, the roads would often get washed away. Ashish travelled either by scooter, cycle or bullock cart, or sometimes even walked, to carry out door-to-door visits to check on his patients.

Apart from nature's challenges, there were other challenges in store, too. Once at midnight, a patient suffering heart attack was admitted to the government hospital in Dharni. The government hospital did not have any specialists and Ashish was called to treat the patient. This hospital did not have adequate facilities and Ashish only had an ECG machine and the injection Streptokinase. It was a 'do or die' moment for Ashish and he recalls thinking at that time, *I can try to treat the patient with my meagre resources, but if I am unsuccessful and he succumbs, then people will never believe that I had tried my best. If there is a death in my hands, I might have to leave Melghat. On the bright side, if I treat this patient, there is*

*still a 90% chance that he will be saved, but if left untreated, there is
100% chance of death.* He came out of this dilemma with the
firm resolve to take the risk and started the treatment. He sat
by the patient's side for the next four hours until at around 4
am, the patient slowly started showing signs of improvement.
Five days later, he recovered fully and was discharged from
the hospital. This marked the beginning of people's faith in
Ashish's treatment.

In 1998, a few months after he established MAHAN,
Ashish married Kavita, who was doing her MS in ophthalmic
surgery at that time. When the marriage proposal was
brought to Ashish, his only condition was that Kavita first
visits Melghat and decides if she could lead a life in those
inhospitable conditions and work for the tribal communities.
Kavita visited Melghat, saw the hospital and happily and
wholeheartedly agreed to be a part of this challenging life.
In 2001, after completing her MS, Kavita shifted to Melghat
and started an eye hospital under MAHAN Trust.

Due to the very simple life they led, they could purchase
an operating microscope with their savings. Gradually they
started receiving financial support from individuals, KHS,
Caring Friends Mumbai, etc., and improved the hospital
facilities.

Melghat's forests are famous for its wildlife consisting of
tigers and poisonous snakes. Initially, Kavita was afraid for
Ashish's life as he went about his patient visits travelling
through these dangerous routes. Understanding her worry,
Ashish's elder brother Avinash donated his jeep, because of
which they were able to extend their medical relief work to
the more interior parts of Melghat.

However, the initial years were quite a disappointment for
Kavita's ophthalmology practice due to the superstitions and
ignorance of the local people. The tribal men and women
believed that doctors, in the name of eye surgery, would
replace the human eye with an eye from a dead animal! The
frustrating lack of patients with eye ailments left Kavita often

depressed and she would remark sarcastically to Ashish, "I will probably have to operate the cataract of a tiger!" Ultimately, Kavita spent one whole year visiting more than 50 villages in Melghat, conducting door-to-door eye check-ups and spreading awareness about eye treatment among the villagers.

Once during her visits, Kavita didn't get a bus back home so she had to spend the night sleeping outside a tribal hut. They had heard about a tiger attack in that village a few days before. Just before daybreak, Kavita felt a leg resting on her abdomen. She leapt up in fright thinking it was the same tiger and shouted for help. Immediately, she realized her mistake – it was a calf, which had kept his one leg over Kavita and when it heard her screams, it ran away, alarmed.

Around this time, Ashish and Kavita were blessed with a baby boy, Athang. Since there was nobody else to look after the baby, Kavita would carry a swaddled four-month-old Athang along with her for her village visits. She used to keep him in a makeshift cradle suspended from a tree and would set up her outdoor eye camp right next to it. If she had to admit a needy case to their hospital, she would bring back the patient in her own vehicle. Since there was no cook in the hospital, Kavita herself would prepare meals for her patients and feed them. She believes that patient is God and serving the patient is real. In such difficult circumstances, she operated upon many cataract patients and slowly, her reputation spread in the villages.

There is an incident that Ashish fondly remembers about Kavita and he narrates, "Once a pregnant woman was in labour and her condition was critical. Her relatives insisted that Kavita must conduct the delivery. Though Kavita was not an obstetrician, she delivered the baby and saved both the mother and the child. The mother was not lactating and could not nurse her baby. At that time, Kavita was breast-feeding a six-month-old Athang. So she took the selfless decision of giving half of her milk to the newborn baby. I was stunned myself with her decision and thought how incredibly compassionate she was. Kavita is always one step ahead of me; she thinks from her heart."

Ashish and Kavita's relentless dedication and full-time work for the villagers often left them facing grave difficulties in their own family life. Once Kavita developed arrhythmia, which caused temporary fainting, but she didn't abandon Melghat and continued her work. Another time, Athang developed a high fever at night and had severe abdominal pain. With his painful condition, there was no way they could have taken him to a specialized hospital in the nearest city of Amaravati, which was 140 km away. So Ashish preferred to rely on his own clinical judgment, referred paediatric books and started the treatment. By the next morning, Athang felt better and they heaved a sigh of relief. Another time, Athang suffered a serious ear inflammation due to a ruptured ear and he experienced excruciating pain throughout the night. As there was no ENT surgeon in Melghat, Ashish again treated him at home and Athang recovered by morning.

All these episodes made Ashish think, "We both are highly qualified doctors but unfortunately, we cannot provide expert paediatric facilities to our own son in Melghat. We have to come out of our own personal comfort zone to serve the nation, even if it is at the cost of family life."

Hearing about the death of the tribal widow's malnourished son suffering from pneumonia, and about the deaths of five children due to diarrhoea, Kavita and Ashish were acutely saddened and unable to sleep for nights. Melghat, at that time, had appallingly high malnutrition figures and infant mortality rates. Kavita demanded Ashish to arrange health camps in different villages to stop such untimely deaths of children. But Ashish realized that the need of the hour was quite different because of the large area and limited availability of resources. Thus was born the idea of barefoot doctors trained with medical knowledge, chosen from amongst the illiterate tribal community.

During that time, Ashish was convinced of the 'replicability' of the home-based neonatal care approach developed by Dr. Abhay Bang of SEARCH (Society for Education, Action and Research in Community Health), in Melghat. MAHAN Trust adopted 38 villages and trained illiterate and semi-literate tribal women as village health workers (VHWs) for treatment of childhood illnesses. Till date, these VHWs have treated more than 1,05,000 patients, reduced child deaths and curbed malnutrition by 64% and adult deaths by 42%. There have been several remarkable cases demonstrating the dedication of VHWs who saved babies suffering from birth asphyxia by giving them artificial respiration, who have rescued a baby from neonatal sepsis and who have saved a severely malnourished girl suffering from pneumonia with the help of drugs and ready-to-use therapeutic food.

"Many a time, we have saved very critical heart attack or brain haemorrhage patients in the absence of electricity, using just candles."
~ Dr. Asish Satav

The concept of barefoot doctors started gaining good results and MAHAN's project received the Young Scientist Award and Best Tribal Health Research Project Award from the Indian Council of Medical Research. Their research work has been showcased in many international journals, conferences and even the Indian government has implemented many of Ashish's recommendations as state-level policies.

However in spite of such selfless work being done for the community, Ashish faced all kinds of opposition. In 2004-2005, MAHAN Trust raised the issue of malnutrition via newspaper and TV and highlighted many lacunae and negligence of government's health department and Integrated Child Development Services programme, who in turn, reacted with anger and threatened Ashish. A few people tried to lodge fake police complaints and court cases against him. One of MAHAN's VHW from Kokmar village was pressurized by government workers to stop her work. When Ashish went to the village to look into the matter, the villagers were reluctant to talk to him as they were told that MAHAN was defaming their village by publishing names of the severely malnourished babies.

A little while after, Ashish saw a thin boy walking past clutching a roti in his hand and immediately recognized him as the malnourished child who had come to his notice three months ago. The poor child had been bedridden and was not even getting proper nutrition from the government-run *anganwadis.* Since MAHAN had published his name in the newspapers, the government had taken notice of his plight and had started providing him special diet and healthcare, due to which he had slowly recovered. When Ashish explained this fact to the villagers, they realized their misconception and started supporting MAHAN. Thus, the particular VHW could resume her work.

Experts from Rajmata Jijau Mother and Children Health and Nutrition mission of Maharashtra government and United Nations Children's Fund (UNICEF), personally visited their project area, verified MAHAN's findings on prevailing malnutrition and children mortality, and left satisfied with MAHAN's survey reports. They started measures to improve the situation as per MAHAN's recommendations and eventually, the government started cooperating with them. On MAHAN's request, local tribal youths were appointed as counsellors in all government hospitals. This programme is being jointly run as a partnership between government and voluntary agencies.

Ashish and Kavita faced all pressure tactics and opposition courageously. In January 2012, Ashish was informed by their lawyer that he had been charged with conspiracy to murder and that he would be arrested within the next few days. At that time, MAHAN had organized an eye surgery camp where 30 blind patients and others with eye problems from the interiors of Melghat and Madhya Pradesh were to be operated. In the face of the arrest-threat, Ashish asked Kavita to either postpone the camp or shift the patients elsewhere for surgeries. But Kavita was firm and told Ashish, "All these patients are very poor and they cannot afford to go anywhere else. So I will conduct the camp and manage the hospital even if you get arrested." In that moment, Ashish thought, *I am so lucky to have such a dedicated and fearless wife. She is a true life partner ready to bear all shocks of my life without any complaints and with full acceptance.* Kavita successfully conducted the camp and ultimately it was proven that all those charges were baseless. Ashish did not get arrested.

When Ashish got angry due to such false allegations, one of his friends and well-wishers, Dr. Avinash Saoji, advised him to follow the teaching of Acharya Vinoba Bhave: "Fight the sword with the shield and not with the sword itself." With these words, Ashish changed his strategy and started improving MAHAN's rapport within the community by increasing community participation in the project. Eventually, they opposed all those anti-social elements who were threatening Ashish. In Ashish's own words, "I think, these obstacles are not hurdles in the road, but challenges that test us to prove ourselves. Life is like a river which is even more beautiful when it flows through mountains, valleys and falls."

While running the MAHAN trust, Ashish has worn many hats apart from just that of a physician. To provide a sustainable solution to malnutrition, Ashish developed 3,500 kitchen gardens in the homes of these villagers and started intensive communication programmes.

Today, MAHAN has been included in several committees for deciding policies on malnutrition reduction in Maharashtra. Ashish has won several awards for his contributions, like the Karmaveer Puraskaar, the Real Award by Save the Children International, the Spirit of Humanity Award by Americare Foundation, etc.

Speaking of the daily hardships he faces in carrying out

his work in Melghat, Ashish comments, "Lack of water and electricity in Dharni is routine for us. Very high temperatures up to 48 degrees during summers, cold waves with the temperature reaching 3 degrees during winters and incessant heavy rains during the rainy season leading to floods, isolating villages from Dharni and other towns; all these are now routine for us. Many a time, we have saved very critical heart attack or brain haemorrhage patients in the absence of electricity, using just candles." He goes on to say, "In the beginning, people were suspicious whether an MD doctor can stay in such inhospitable and extreme conditions or would he run away within months. On the other hand, I had doubts about whether tribal patients would accept me. At first, very few patients came to me for treatment, but I continued my medical care without becoming depressed. When I treated and saved serious patients with brain haemorrhage, heart attack, cerebral malaria and meningitis, people developed confidence in me and I slowly started getting recognized. Now those tribals who visit me usually become my permanent patients and I become their family doctor."

The first couple of years of running the hospital were an endless struggle. Due to a lack of trained staff, Ashish initially managed everything single-handedly with the help of a 9th standard-pass youth.

Today, MAHAN has treated more than 68,000 patients in the hospital and OPD, conducted specialty camps for 17,500 patients, performed free of cost plastic surgery on more than 464 burn victims, treated more than 40,000 adults under mortality control programme and provided vision to more 10,000 patients. Their advocacy has resulted in eight policy changes by the government which has benefitted more than five lakh children. What started with one attendant in a rudimentary hospital has now grown to a team of four doctors, nurses, midwives and attendants, working in a hospital with equipment like cardiac monitor, ventilators, defibrillator and sophisticated eye examination machines.

Ashish summarises MAHAN's future with these words, "MAHAN's future plans are to build a new hospital with an ICU and an advanced eye care hospital. My goal is to conduct further community-based research on malnutrition and addiction in Melghat, replicate MAHAN's model in all tribal areas of Maharashtra and be an advisor for national health policies for tribal parts of India related to malnutrition, mortality and eye health. I dream of making MAHAN the best tribal area health institute in India. All of MAHAN's achievements have been possible only due to continuous support from Caring Friends, Kasturba Health Society and the blessings of my parents. Despite the difficulties and hurdles, we have never felt frustrated so as to leave Melghat. It is the greatest achievement of our lives."

Biographer

Jeroninio "Jerry" Almeida is a celebrated inspirational speaker, author, teacher, executive coach, social crusader, UN advisor and internationally-certified leadership training expert. His purpose is to awaken the HERO and champions of change within each of us and create widespread change.

moJOsh Inspirator Power 3:
The Power of Resourcefulness

"However desperate the situation and circumstances, don't despair. When there is everything to fear, be unafraid. When surrounded by dangers, fear none of them. When without resources, depend on resourcefulness. When surprised, take the enemy by surprise."

~ Sun Tzu

Thought Leadership for Reflection: Many people have a lot and more of resources, but do not do or achieve much because they do not have the resourcefulness to do anything worthwhile with what they have. All resources are useless when you do not have the resourcefulness to be useful.

Ideas for Action: Try and always think of ideas to make things happen with less or nothing. Your integrity and dignity will help you to become resourceful and find solutions to any and all concerns. But do it in the right way. Resourcefulness is your ability to be ingenious, capable, and full of initiative, especially in dealing with difficult situations and concerns. Test yourself to be resourceful in all difficult situations to push your potential.

4

Carving One's Own Path with a Thums Up to Life

Ashok Kurien

Do we call Ashok Kurien the ad man who changed the pattern of Indian advertising? Or as one of the first to recognize the potential of private television channels? Do we call him a serial entrepreneur par excellence? Do we call him a swell motivational speaker? Do we call him a person who thrives to innovate and learn continuously? Like many remarkable achievers and trendsetters, he is all of this and more.

Ashok Kurien is the founder of Ambience Advertising that has had many successful ones, Garden Vareli; Thums Up; Saffola; Lakme; Kamasutra; Parachute and P&G and many other highly successful campaigns. Not just this, he is also the co-founder of Zee TV, the premier private television channel in India, and is a serial entrepreneur today.

This is a success story for sure, but when we know more about his life, he will surely make us sit up in surprise and awe.

Ashok Kurien had, what he now calls, 'learning differences'. At that time, which was the 1960s, a different pattern of learning was not understood at all by anyone. As a result of that, Ashok was labelled a failure and an irresponsible young boy by all his teachers.

Ashok's family was from a middle-income group where education was considered extremely important. He had, in fact, got into an elite school, because his mother was a teacher there, and on a scholarship for poor Christian students. But unfortunately, his mother too was ignorant about different patterns in learning.

To Ashok, education at school became irrelevant and boring. Finding everything difficult, he would often daydream during classes. Talking about those days, he says, "Now there are educational systems which say, 'Oh, there is a creative product! This is a kid with some amazing imagination.' Now there are teachers who pick up that imagination and take the child in the right direction. In those days, if you were a dreamer, you were not good, because nobody knew what was dyslexia, what was ADS (attention deficiency syndrome) and nobody recognized creativity."

Corporal punishment was quite common in that era, and therefore, he was caned and punished at school and even at home. Regular beatings turned him into a rebel. Ashok failed in the 7th standard and then 9th standard. His rebellious and aggressive nature also led him to alcohol and drugs. However, there was one area he excelled in – sports. In fact, the reason he was not thrown out of school was because he was the sports captain, the gym captain and the boxing captain.

After completing school, Ashok got admission in Elphinstone College, but after failing the first year exams, he ran away from home. He got a job with a crop spraying company, Helicopter Services, where his job was to bribe government employees every day for various certificates. He lived in villages all over India, especially South India, for three years, sleeping on the floor, in the back of a truck or under a tree. By the end of the third year, he was so depressed that he was ready to jump into a river and commit suicide.

Fortunately, this did not happen and realization struck him. He understood that the only way to achieve anything was to get a degree, so he returned to Mumbai and enrolled in college. Whilst studying, he was doing odd jobs, sticking stamps at the Institute of Bankers for ₹7 per day and selling advertising space for *Debonair* magazine. He attempted one subject at a time and did his best.

As Ashok took his last exam, which was Hindi, one of the first miracles in his life took place – the invigilator took pity on him and substituted his blank answer sheet for one already completed. This was a miracle for sure, for the only reason, the man, Arun Thomas, helped him was because he had once been Ashok's mother's student. Twenty-six years later, Ashok ran into Arun, who told him that he had never broken his principles before or since, but that an 'inner voice' at that moment had urged him to help the youngster out.

Ashok's real education was always through observing life in all its dimensions, step by step. Working at *Debonair*, Ashok had learnt how to sell and this actually led to his first office job with the advertising agency, Rediffusion. Here, he heard terms like 'marketing strategy' and 'brand building' for the first time. He started noticing the quality that he did have, which was the ability to break down a problem into the simplest form and finding a creative solution. He, in fact, had the skill to make bottom-up solutions and turn them into top-down strategies and campaigns, which made his clients very happy.

> Ashok's real education was always through observing life in all its dimensions, step by step. Working at Debonair, Ashok had learnt how to sell and this actually led to his first office job with the advertising agency, Rediffusion.

Shilpa Shah of Garden Sarees convinced Ashok into starting his own advertising agency with her company as its flagship account. "Shilpa believed in me," Ashok states, "and that motivated me a great deal." With little resources and pressing family needs, the plunge was risky and the fall, too deep – particularly as the late 80s were marked by slow economic growth rates. "You have to be either very brave or very stupid to start your own venture. I was extremely stupid, with such little money!" laughs Ashok. His client's belief in him gave birth to Ambience Advertising. Ashok calls it 'the true learning of entrepreneurship', as 'the buck truly stops with you.'

Thus, in 1987, with around ₹5,000 in his pocket, Ashok set

up Ambience Advertising, *his first defining moment,* bringing in the brilliant art director Elsie Nanji as a partner.

Seeing some Asian countries abandon traditional attire for Western wear, he persuaded Garden Sarees to also make salwar kameez fabric, boosting its revenue and launching the Vareli brand.

The second defining moment for Ashok was a campaign that rocketed him and Ambience to fame in its very first year itself. It was done for its second client, Thums Up, called 'Thums Up - Taste the Thunder'. After 25 successful years, it is easily among the longest-running national campaigns in India. Once again, Ashok attributes this to a brave client, one who trusted him. This time it was Ramesh Chauhan, the promoter of Thums Up (and Bisleri). "Ramesh gave me the opportunity to come up with the entire business strategy of the 'Maha Cola'". Back then, Thums Up and Campa Cola were the only two major colas in the market. Ramesh Chauhan gave Ashok and his agency complete freedom to draw up not just the communication, but also a product and business plan for Thums Up. "Very few people trust you like that," Ashok says.

Ashok visited Thums Up's Mumbai, Delhi and Punjab plants. He involved himself in every aspect of the product – from changing the shape and size of the bottles, to their cost and ingredients, to a complete marketing, business and communication analysis. "This was my self-awakening to my vision, talent and understanding of the Indian consumer," he says.

"We wiped out Campa Cola – from a 60% market share to a brand of the past," recalls Ashok, who currently is an advisor to Bisleri (promoted by Ramesh Chauhan, again) and was behind Bisleri's re-launch (including a change in the brand's colour from blue to green). "The Thums Up experience gave me the confidence to evolve strategic marketing and new business solutions. It took me beyond advertising," he adds.

New businesses poured in. Soon, the agency had many

well-known clients: Garden Vareli, Thums Up, Saffola, Lakme, Kamasutra, Citibank, Parachute, Nestle and P&G.

In 1992, four years after he started Ambience, one of Ashok's clients, Subhash Chandra of Essel World Amusement Parks, was talking about television when he suddenly said, "Why can't we do something like this in India, that is, start a private television channel?" Those were the days when Doordarshan ruled TV, and Ashok himself had dabbled with the creation of some shows, including *Nukkad*. Satellite TV was unheard of.

Subhash invited Ashok to join him as a partner to look after marketing and sales. Zee TV was launched and went on to become a huge success. "Subhash could have got anyone he chose to partner his dream to launch satellite TV in India. But he said he wanted me on it," recollects Ashok.

Ashok Kurien then helped found Dish TV, India. com and other ventures, so he now started being called a serial entrepreneur. Every three years or so, he has found something new to start and says, "I never do anything on my own. I always have a partner. The one truth in partnership is that if your partner's strengths are your weaknesses and if your partner's weaknesses are your strengths, then you have a team that is exceptionally powerful, because there is no conflict." It's only positive energy.

Learning about Learning

Most of us would agree that until we understand who we are – our strengths and weaknesses in totality – achieving anything in life on our own strength is impossible.

Ashok understood and recognized this much later in life. He was of course born in an era, where things like dyslexia were not understood. He, however, did succeed in life, despite many struggles because he did not give up and also kept questioning life.

He says, "There is no such thing as a learning disability, some of us 'learn differently'. I learnt in the villages, on the streets of Mumbai, from my experiences. I can't use big words, but I can still learn." Ashok learnt that his true calling lay in converting his real-life observations into business ideas.

While recently talking about the importance of asking 'Why' at TedEx, Ashok reiterated what he tells everyone, that we should never be afraid to say that we don't know or understand something. Only then do people simplify things for us and then get to the crux of the matter. With this kind of attitude, we will save time and energy, and develop the ability to see the core issue and ignore the complications.

When he started earning reasonably well, he wanted to give some of it away. He found it hard to fathom that from a position of having no money and being in debt, in one year he could have plentiful.

He recommends this to everyone in life. "Question, listen and learn all the time', he says, "the truly educated never graduate."

Back in his office, Ashok points to the posters of boxing legend Muhammad Ali and Olympian sprinter Carl Lewis. He says: "Everything I've learnt about life is right here. When you are going to fight, stand there and win. There are no draws in boxing." He laughs. "When you know you are going to lose, learn how to run... real fast!"

Ashok now finds himself in constant demand for advice: from businessmen to parents who have children with learning differences. He also has given talks in many such schools and had numerous one-on-one meetings. Belnera Fernandes, a parent at JBCN Pan Academy, says, "Ashok Kurien's courage in sharing his failures with us is a real inspiration."

He sets aside at least a few hours every week to simply listen and advise any young person who asks for career or business guidance, and gives them his full attention.

"For anyone who had problems like mine, it needed just one person, to say, I believe in you, because it helped me believe in myself," Ashok shares and motivates people by further telling them, "The day you believe in yourself, you can do anything."

Giving and Sharing

Despite facing many challenges in life, Ashok had succeeded. He also understood he loved helping others, as it did always make him feel better.

One incident he remembers and considers one of the turning points in his life is during his time at Rediffusion. He was on the bus on his way to work and had just ₹100, for the rest of the month, in his pocket. He saw a poor, physically disabled man struggling to find the change for his bus fare. When he stepped off the bus, he put his last ₹100 into the shirt pocket of this man. Reflecting on that day, Ashok says, "It may be the only time that I gave all that I had as my inner voice told me that this man needed it more than I did." This made Ashok understand that charity is not only about money but about understanding the plight of another human being.

When he started earning reasonably well, he wanted to give some of it away. He found it hard to fathom that from a position of having no money and being in debt, in one year he could have plentiful. He had come into contact with a rehabilitation centre for street alcoholics called Mary's Clan, started by Cyril D'Souza, a recovered alcoholic himself, at Mount Mary in Bandra. As someone close and dear to him had suffered from alcoholism earlier, Ashok started supporting them.

On the professional side, when Zee went public in 1995, Ashok started giving larger donations to organizations that he came across and needed help. He also made a list of all needy families and friends' children and gifted them all shares in the company.

Ashok started donating ad hoc to causes close to him, drug and alcohol addiction of particular note. Later, he established his own trust, The Ammada Trust, in 2002, with the help and advice of close family and friends, to donate in a more systematic way.

The geographical focus of Ammada Trust is Maharashtra and it started funding individuals for health and education. Ashok's cousin, Arjun Menon, runs the trust. Ashok's involvement has become more hands-on: visiting projects and looking at long-term solutions to social issues. Ashok says that the trigger to his more focused giving came when he met his present wife, who works in development, and taught him the adage that giving a man a fish will feed him for a day, but teaching a man to fish will feed him for a lifetime.

Ashok has also more recently become involved with the organizations Give India, Social Venture Partners and Dasra, which are encouraging more strategic philanthropy in India from individuals who are able to give back to the society. These individuals are focused on addressing social issues and challenges that can be scaled up through organizations, which are doing great work in their areas but need specific financial and management expertise in order to grow and reach more people. Ashok recognizes the need for organizations like these that help manage social investment, so that the investor knows what his funding is achieving.

At the age of 67, his latest business venture is a culmination of all this. Livinguard is a company that aims to give the poor pure and safe bacteria and virus-free drinking water at a very low cost. Ashok feels he has found the purpose of his life, using his business acumen to earn money as well as use it for the good of others.

He has installed these Livinguard Water Filters in over 30,000 village homes in Maharashtra and Gujarat at a cost of ₹800 to ₹950 each. The 500 community filters that they have placed in rural schools and hospitals at just ₹40,000 to ₹1,00,000 each and low cost of maintenance. With even electricity not being mandatory to run these filters, it is an ideal tool for India. With Livinguard, they have already touched the lives of 25 million poor people and have an ambitious target to reach out to 50 million poor people by the end of 2017. To make it easier for them, Ashok personally campaigns to companies to support this remarkable tool through their Company Social Responsibility (CSR) initiatives.

The proof of the pudding is in the eating. Now, in the rural areas, the attendance has gone up by 15-20% in the schools and the village *sarpanch* says no one suffered from illness right through the monsoon ever since these Livinguard filters were installed. An agreement recently entered with a multinational company partner promises to take this low cost technology to over half a billion people around the world.

Ashok is also the co-inventor of the world's first washable, reusable, bacteria/yeast killing/non-leaking sanitary napkins. "We hope to touch the lives of three billion girls/women around the world who cannot afford sanitary napkins," he says about the product.

Ashok feels this is truly the most rewarding thing he has done in his life, but knowing him, I am sure there will be many more such game changers to come.

He concludes by saying, "I have been blessed with more opportunities than most people in this country and I have been blessed with more success."

Biographers

Jamuna Rangachari is a software professional and writer who currently manages the websites of *Life Positive* and also writes for the magazine. She has authored three books for children, compiled and interpreted *Teaching Stories I* and *Teaching Stories II* for Life Positive and published a book titled *Dancing with Life: Living with Multiple Sclerosis.* Her articles have also been published in *Daily News and Analysis, New Woman, Khabar* (an NRI magazine), *Wedding Vows* and the *Times of India* among others. She also blogs at www.jai-joy.com.

Rachel Wawn is passionate and committed to a more socially responsible world, with a Master's in governance and development from Institute of Development Studies, UK. She recently produced Footsteps4Good, a charity fun run in Mumbai. Rachel is currently working with a group of women at an NGO on a livelihood project, as well as helping two other NGOs that are focussed on preparing Indian youth to be 'job ready'.

moJOsh Inspirator Power 4:
The Power of Humility

"What are human beings so arrogant about? Our origin is a sperm, our end is a carcass and in between we are a vessel for excrement. "

~ Imam Ali

Thought Leadership for Reflection: Humility is treating a minister, priest, teacher, waiter, janitor, homosexual, transgender and every human being with equal and mutual respect. Remember these words when you feel angry or upset towards anyone: "I further clarify that no matter who I am speaking with or even giving feedback to because something has irritated me; I need to have the integrity to do it with dignity and be resourceful to give feedback in the right way."

Ideas for Action: Human beings by design cannot be humble. Our basic DNA is flawed. What a lot of humans call humility, is what I call The Statue of Humility, which, like the statue of liberty, is just a symbol but the humility and liberty are superficial. That's why human beings are very reverent when they are speaking with a priest or a guru in a temple or a holy place but not as respectful when they are speaking with their house help. We are respectful while speaking with the boss but not as respectful with someone who reports to us. Have the integrity to practice giving equal and same respect to one and all.

5

The Musical Journey of a Special Child

Benzy Kumar

Benzy Kumar, a special child, needs no introduction today. Diagnosed with intellectual disability and cerebral palsy, has demonstrated her strength, determination and the unfathomable power of music. She has won several accolades, including two national awards, Zee Astitva Award, Karamveer Puraskaar, Limca Book of Records certificate and many other laurels. Though so young, Benzy has many musical albums to her credit today. But there was a time when she was a cause for concern to everyone in the family. She could not speak, let alone sing. Doctors were pessimistic about her very survival. But proving everybody wrong, Benzy, the destiny's child, has carved a special name in the vast ocean of music. She has grown into a singing sensation and an inspiration to many.

In December 1992, Kavita Kumar became the mother of a beautiful baby girl. But all was not well with the baby and she had to be put in the incubator. Outside, India was at the peak of a communal frenzy post the Babri Masjid demolition. In Kavita's neighbourhood, too, there was nervousness and tension. But Kavita had her own worries. "With every call from the doctor, my heart used to sink further," recollects Kavita. This continued for 40 days.

After this trial period, Kavita and her newborn daughter came home and everybody was jubilant. The occasion was duly celebrated. The baby brought happiness and smiles on the faces of both sets of grandparents. They named the little girl Benzy – "excellent son" in Hebrew (original meaning is 'the son of Zion'). In Brazil, Benzy is the name of a flower that blooms once in 20 years. Kavita and her husband were most content.

But after three or four months, Kavita realized that her little Benzy was not as active as the other babies of the same age. It disturbed her. And when the child showed no signs of development, she convinced her husband, Praveen Kumar, to take the baby for a proper medical examination. They decided to take their child to a renowned child specialist, Dr. Malik, in Lucknow. On the day of their appointment, they prayed, gave silent acknowledgement to each other's unsaid fears and doubts, and courageously entered the clinic.

Dr. Malik examined the little baby and without mincing words, yet cautiously, pronounced his judgment, "She is a 'special child'. Her left side is completely stiff and even the brain is damaged."

The bubble of happiness burst.

Kavita and Praveen's invisible fears had taken form and shape. The truth hung in front of them like an ugly, black and white sketch. As long as they didn't know the truth, there was hope. But now knowing what it is with certainty shattered them.

"His words completely numbed us. We were devastated. We didn't know what to say and how to console each other. While driving back, my husband caught hold of my hand and said, 'Don't worry, Kavita; we'll work out something. We will go to Delhi or Mumbai or wherever is necessary and provide our baby with the best treatment possible.' And we also decided not to talk about Benzy's condition at home, to anyone," Kavita recounts the incident with moist eyes.

At home, they put up a brave front, not letting their emotions betray them. Kavita and Praveen decided to take Benzy to the Spastics Society of India in Mumbai that is supported by the Nargis Dutt Foundation. This visit proved to be a revelation. It changed their world, their perspective, their thinking. "It was a completely different world. There were so many children suffering similar condition as Benzy. We took extensive training on how to bring up such children. Stimulant therapy, in particular, was an eye opener," Kavita recalls.

Seeing so many special children around, it kindled a ray of hope in them, and reinforced their belief and faith in themselves to provide a meaningful life to Benzy. It was a moment of truth, of reality, of self-realization, of decision, that dawned upon them.

They took a decision. They decided *not* to have another child; they decided to give Benzy, their special child, all the attention. They also resolved to make her as self-reliant as possible. And from that moment, Kavita's life and mission became a one-point chartered agenda – to take care of her daughter and to bring awareness in the society and among parents of special children.

Kavita gave up her job. Praveen took a transfer to Delhi and even forfeited his promotion in the process. Everybody in the family was against their decision. Their friends, too, ridiculed them. But they stuck to their resolve. In 1995, all three – Kavita, Praveen and Benzy shifted to Delhi and began their life's journey with a fresh perspective.

Initially, people didn't like Kavita bringing Benzy along during social gatherings, but Kavita would not leave Benzy at home. She was not ashamed, frightened or conscious of what people said about her.

Benzy became Kavita and Praveen's world. Needs of special children became their all-pervasive concern. Kavita reminisces, "I was not bothered about relatives or friends anymore. My world was Benzy, and other such children and their parents."

Initially, people didn't like Kavita bringing Benzy along during social gatherings, but Kavita would not leave Benzy at home. She was not ashamed, frightened or conscious of what people said about her. Consequently, everybody avoided her. She became an outcast.

But all this did not deter the couple. They boycotted whosoever had grudges against them for bringing Benzy to social functions. They admitted Benzy in the best Delhi schools – first Step by Step School and then to Sri Ram School. About 75% of their income was spent on Benzy.

Kavita had heard about the impact of music therapy. She decided to experiment with it. But the question was 'How?' The tragedy was that Benzy had no voice at all. But in 1997, Kavita noticed that Benzy responded to music. After continued close observation, she noticed Benzy's eyeballs moving along with the music produced by a toy. She played the musical toy again and again. Benzy smiled and her pupils moved. This kindled a ray of hope in Kavita's heart.

She decided to bring positivity and harmony in her daughter's life through musical notes and immediately bought many musical toys. She would play them near Benzy and the child would listen to the music attentively. It confirmed Kavita's belief that music could do wonders. She researched about music therapy and consulted her husband. Both of them decided to appoint a guru who could teach Benzy musical notes. It was an arduous task as Benzy was a restless child who would not sit at one place for long and would not listen to commands or respect the expectations of a teacher. She would do things according to her mood. But Kavita was determined. She knew music could and will help Benzy fight her ailment. She approached many music teachers before M. M. Rafiq, an old guru, agreed to take up the challenge.

Initially, it was a disaster. The guru repeatedly complained of wastage of time and money as Benzy would not sit with him like other students to learn patiently. His patience was being tested, every day, every minute. Many a time, he threatened to leave, but Kavita persuaded him to stay on. She requested him to come, sing musical notes and try to teach Benzy. She knew it was difficult, but not impossible. Somewhere she knew that this was the only way to make music seep through her daughter's intellect and her heart. Ultimately, the patience paid off. After two years of grueling sessions, at the age of six, Benzy began to sing. Music started to attract her. She was drawn towards it. Her voice also became clearer, louder and melodious.

Yet, the road ahead was wary and frightening. But Kavita was determined. Her sporting background and a sportsperson's motto of 'never giving up' always came to her rescue whenever she felt discouraged. At the age of seven, Benzy play keyboard along with singing. Now Kavita wanted her daughter to perform on stage, but no event management company was prepared to take the risk of putting a special child on stage.

Once again, she was dejected, but she was not defeated.

She was determined to showcase her special child's musical talent. She decided to record Benzy singing. And once again, she hit a boulder. It was difficult to force Benzy to sing in a studio environment, with headphones on and giving retakes. Benzy refused to see her mother's point of view. She did not record. So, Kavita devised an alternate strategy. She recorded as many as ten ragas at one go, without any retakes, without headphones. She titled it 'Basic Ragas'. This was Benzy's first foray into the musical world. But before launching it, Kavita sent this album to various well-known musicians for comments. "Only Shubha Mudgal replied, saying that the child had potential. And her words further strengthened my faith in my daughter," Kavita recollects.

It was encouraging for the parents.

In 2000, once again, destiny tested Kavita's nerve. Ataxia struck her husband who had been her support and her strength. Ataxia is the lack of muscle coordination that affects speech, eye movements and many other body functions. Now she had to look after him as well as Benzy. It was a challenging time, but Kavita's never-say-die attitude and a deep sense of optimism revived her spirits. And Benzy's foray into music was just taking wings.

Today, Benzy can sing classical bhajans, film songs and various ragas. Throughout the day, she is engrossed in music – either singing or playing on her 75-key synthesizer with professional precision or listening to music on the computer. After *Basic Ragas*, her next album *Koshish* was the first experiment in which Benzy sang on a music track. It was released by Bollywood actor Hritik Roshan. He profusely praised her parents and her guru for helping Benzy find her meaning in life.

Following this, came two more albums – *Shakti* and *Benzy Instrumental.* And in 2008, her album, *Ashaayein,* was blessed by no lesser personality than Lata Mangeshkar. After listening to *Ashaayein,* Lata Mangeshkar said: "*Benzy ki* CD *suni. Mujhe bahut achchi lagi. Jo bachi baat nahi ker sakti wo gana itne achche terike se gaa sakti hai. Mujhe aashcharye huya. Mera aashirwad sada iske saath hai.*" (Heard Benzy's CD. I liked it. The child who cannot talk is able to sing so well! I am amazed. My blessings are always with Benzy.)

After two years of grueling sessions, at the age of six, Benzy began to sing. Music started to attract her. She was drawn towards it.

In this album, Benzy has given voice to her mother's lyrics, which try to capture the emotions a special child may not otherwise be able to express.

Music made Benzy confident. She is not frightened of the crowd or of performing live shows anymore. In 2007, a programme, 'Benzy Nite', was organized in Surya Auditorium, Lucknow. Attended by thousands of people, the concert featured Benzy as the main artiste. She sang for hours, rendering one song after the other, not at all shy or hesitant. She even sang duets with professional singers.

But in 2010, Benzy's life changed again. Her anchor, guide and support, passed away. Her father died after battling a long illness. It was shattering for both mother and daughter. "He was our source of strength," says Kavita, with tears welling up in her eyes.

Her father's death had a profound impact on Benzy. She withdrew into a shell. She stopped singing or meeting people. Smile vanished from her face. All day, she would just sit around, staring at the blank walls. When Kavita saw this, she forgot her pain, mustered her strength and began to concentrate completely on Benzy, once again. She began to infuse fresh vigour, confidence and self-belief in her daughter to brave the odds. She made it a point to create an atmosphere at home where Benzy could start her singing again, feel secure and forget the pain of losing her father. After remaining in her own world for nearly two years, now once again Benzy has resumed singing. "It took some time for me and for her to come to grips with the situation but now I am just giving my full attention to Benzy," says Kavita. She is planning Benzy's next album and has already begun work on it.

In the words of Anandji, the renowned music director, "Today Benzy Kumar needs no introduction. She is a singing sensation. Try talking to her and she will look through you. She will keep singing or humming. Music is her life, her passion, her source of strength; her fingers keep tapping the table, giving taal to the song. She will not sit for too long at a place. Always on her feet, pacing up and down with her head down, thinking and engrossed in music – her spiritual calling."

Biographer

For Kavita Kumar, it started with the determination of a mother to create a place for her special daughter in the society, and later on translated to total devotion for empowering kids with special needs. She is the Founder General Secretary of Dhoon Foundation, an organization that aims to search, nurture, develop and promote art, music and dance talent in differently abled children and underprivileged budding artists. She is the winner of many awards, like the Zee Astitva Awards for Rare Achievement and Yami Award by the Music Today Group for the best and true dedicated mother of the country. She has also received Civil Society Karmaveer Puruskaar – Disability in 2011.

moJOsh Inspirator Power 5:
The Power of Contentment

"Be Content with what you have; rejoice in the way things are. When you realize there is nothing lacking, the whole world belongs to you."

~ Lao Tzu

Thought Leadership for Reflection: Most people in our world are not enjoying what they have today in the anticipation of wanting more tomorrow. Most people do not even know what they really need or want and are always wanting more than what other people in their neighbourhood, friend circle or family have. In the process, they never even live their life and are always living the neighbour's life or the life of an extended family member or friend.

Ideas for Action: One can never be truly happy inside-out and have peace of mind without having the integrity for understanding contentment. Map your needs and wants. Remember that real happiness is not in the materialistic external things, because happiness truly is in being content and understanding what we need and regulating our wants.

6

Charity Begins at Home

Chiro Priyo Mitra

Life goes on, with pain and happiness in tandem. Chiro Priyo knew this because he has faced many trials and tribulations in life. However, he realized that to empathize with the pain of a complete stranger and do the little bit required to mitigate his suffering and bring happiness into the stranger's life was his karma; and it brought moksha probably for both. He wondered, "Is this what makes us human?" Two souls, far apart in life's intricate web were brought by the arrow of time to meet under the most unfavorable conditions that changed their lives for the better.

Omar (name changed), one among the seven siblings, was born in a poor family in a small village in Uttar Pradesh. They struggled in extreme poverty, but with a caring mother, he and his siblings never had to go empty stomach even for a single night. His father was a daily wage labourer and a drunkard. Whatever they had, his mother made sure that it was shared. Raising so many kids was not easy. But Omar was happy – very happy growing up in the village with not a care in the world. Not having any toys was little deterrent to his happy disposition in life as he rejoiced chasing around the country chicken in his backyard. His mother, however, was worried as pressures mounted with two more kids in tow. The older ones were proving a burden. Putting a heavy stone on her heart, Omar's mother took him to a person in the next village who promised a civilized world for kids of Omar's age with everything – a job, a grand house to live in and employers who would satisfy every need. He also gave two wads of currency notes – which

Omar's mother, even if she couldn't count, knew was enough
to carry the family through two winters. Omar too, though with
a little apprehension, looked forward excitedly with rose-tinted
glasses to the glorious future in the Utopian land. Little did
he know that the 'promise' of 'everything' was just that and
was never meant to be fulfilled. Even the love and care, which
every child needs, and the dignity that every human being
deserves would move further away from him.

Chiro Priyo Mitra was always been happy-go-lucky, growing
under the wings of highly educated parents who instilled
in him a scientific temperament and the values of social
responsibility. He was always tempted to try out in practice
what others would be happy learning in theory – often with
hilarious and sometimes with embarrassing outcomes. His
quixotic ways endeared him to all, justifying the meaning of
his name Chiro Priyo – dear to everybody (lovingly called
Chiro by his friends). His 'doing-it-rather-than-mulling-over-
it' outlook in life took him through great journeys. His career
in veterinary science took him across the world healing the
animals with great zeal. He became a consultant vet with the
United Nations and the European Union. He lived in the US
and Europe for about a decade but then, home beckoned.

Chiro returned to India in 2009 to the National
Capital Region – a futuristic hub in the making dubbed as
'Millennium' city. He married his true love who wrapped up
her work in France as a fashion designer and settled down
in the house she redesigned into a home. Little did Chiro
know, but she began trying to mend Chiro's maverick ways
on the sly.

They were settling down to a blissful life, cruising through it
at a comfortable pace, engrossed in work, catching up with old
friends back from school days and taking up Chiro's passion
for cycling. He restarted his clinical practice at home and got
back to healing the distraught and distressed animals. But little
did he realize that he would be pulled in by the distress of a
child which would change his perspective on life.

On a cold foggy night in December 2010, as they prepared to retire to bed, he and his wife were jolted by the repeated muffled shrieks of a child and the swearing of a hoarse female voice. It paused momentarily but started again with the clamour of utensils, howling of a kid and abuses, which continued for a couple of hours. Chiro with his wife went up the terrace to locate the annoying and disturbing noises but the dense fog made it difficult for them to discern anything. Next day, in the mundane chores of life, the previous night's disturbing events were momentarily pushed to the back of their minds. However, it was short-lived as later that night the wailing, swearing and clamour returned, disturbing the peace. Early next morning, Chiro and his wife went up the stairs again and what they saw shocked them out of their wits. A small, famished kid was out in the cold next door with barely any warm clothing, washing utensils piled up on the culvert in freezing water. Their hearts skipped a few beats when they saw that the kid, on imploring in pain, was being thrashed by a middle-aged woman without any mercy.

> "All these years we have been only taking and exercising our fundamental rights, but now it's time to give back by performing our fundamental duties as diligently as possible."
> ~ Chiro Priyo Mitra

The famished kid was Omar and this was the dream job that he had been offered. Indeed it was a castle of a house with very wealthy and influential owners, but surely not the kingdom he had dreamt of. From the day he had arrived, he had been beaten, starved and tortured. Not only that, he was emotionally drained and hounded. The pet dog of the family who was treated regally was often instigated to bite the boy to instill fear. This had made Omar wish so many times to switch places with the dog.

At night, Omar would cry in muffled voice, afraid to draw the ire of the demonic masters. He longed to run away to his village and to his family but he didn't know where he came from. He was also not sure if the tyrant masters would really catch hold of him and feed him to the dogs, as they had threatened. He resigned to his fate but a little flicker of hope to be freed from this hellhole kept him going.

Chiro and his wife Poonam were momentarily numbed by the sight of the treatment meted out to the child. This was the moment which puts a man at crossroads where he can either choose the hard way and confront the reality or choose the easy way, ignore the events and continue "business as usual". Chiro chose the former. What made him do it? He could have enjoyed the bonhomie of his neighbours and ignored the entire episode, maintaining the tenets of a 'civil society' as many call it. But did the civility extend only to the affluent and influential or did it go beyond the material issues of defining 'human' values of compassion? Being a veterinarian, not only was he compassionate to animals but could also feel their pain. This is what propelled him to work with an untiring sincerity. The thought of a young child being treated worse than even a beast was devastating and shocking.

This prompted Chiro to take up the cudgels against the offenders. The very next morning, he left all his work aside and went up to the neighbours and asked politely if all was well as he had heard cries of a child the previous night coming from their house. He was shown the door unceremoniously with a strong censure to mind his own business. This made him realize that he needed more evidence to substantiate the outrage. The following morning, he captured the inhuman act – the kicking and abusing – on his camcorder as stealthily as he could, risking his life and limb. His ordeal was yet to start as he went pillar to post seeking respite for the tortured soul. At the police station, he was mocked at initially, with the personnel wondering aloud, "You are acting as if Omar is your own child." Then Chiro ran around for a few days hitting his head against an impervious, unyielding wall. He went to the local media who did not see a 'story' worthy enough to stir any economic leverage. But Chiro stood his ground.

This did not deter him though but he still questioned himself – he could turn a blind eye and a deaf ear and get on with his life without getting perturbed but would that justify the education he had received? Was his upbringing only meant to earn money and respect that came with it or did he need the self-respect to look at himself in the mirror without impunity? He says, "One doesn't have to go too far to do something good because charity begins at home."

He did not stop as he was educated not only in the professional sense but because he 'felt' and empathized. He shared his horrible experience with friends and a close friend's wife who was working with a media house. She suggested that they call up a child (abuse) helpline. He called up but without much expectation though.

However, doors open up when you try hard and the unresponsive system he so cursed yielded to his dogged persuasion. An NGO, Shaktivahini, entrusted with the issue of child labour eradication, picked up the case and swung into action. They engaged the police and the media through proper channels and raided the dream house with a warrant.

Omar, already in tatters emotionally and physically, cowered at the sudden hullabaloo, and kept crying expecting more hurt and pain. After a few hours, he realized that he had been rescued. Slowly, he recounted the days of horror. His medical tests showed that the 'concentration camp' had taken its toll – he had chilblains and pneumonia was setting in, but thanks to the timely intervention, it could be treated. He was adopted by the state government. The culprits were booked, but being very rich and powerful they spat and hissed like cornered snakes with some lethal moves. Threats started pouring into Chiro's life and it felt like the ordeal had just started again. At one point of time, his septuagenarian father and Poonam contemplated leaving the city for a safer haven but the cause made them show great *sang-froid* and they stood solid on their ground. The case was not withdrawn even in the face of great discomfiture to Chiro's family. It had its repercussions even later, with their darling family member – a golden retriever – succumbing to malicious poisoning possibly as an upshot to their unwavering stand. Chiro and family still stood firm.

Suddenly, the fourth estate also realized that there was after all a 'story' to be found in the tears of the eight-year-old and plunged in with requests to Chiro for rights to the video footage he had captured. Indeed the sordid and grim footage could do wonders to their TRP. This irked Chiro as he felt utterly disappointed that the value and quality of life is measured in terms of quantifiable deliverables, which ultimately translated into money. But there are elements with noble intentions embedded in the depraved system who try to show the correct picture in the right perspective without any bias. The video eventually went public.

Their hearts skipped a few beats when they saw that the kid, on imploring in pain, was being thrashed by a middle-aged woman, without any mercy.

So Omar got his life back. He later recalled that he often contemplated turning rogue and inflicting harm on his torturers or running away to the end of the world – which he knew not where. Either way a renegade, distressed criminal-to-be or a demented soul, with a fate worse than an animal, had been rescued.

Chiro's actions woke up the Haryana government from slumber and in turn ensured that Omar gets a decent and free schooling. With an eye to his future, they made a fixed deposit in his name, which he will receive on becoming an adult.

Even then, Chiro's mind was not at ease as he wondered about the hundreds of Omars still suffering a similar fate. This led him to pledge a much long-term action. He brainstormed with the NGO and his cycling friends who provided the timely succour and decided on a sustainable option. He fancied if his hobby of cycling would take him towards his goal of spreading awareness and solace. He, with his dedicated group of cyclists, covered a 320-km stretch between Delhi and Ajmer and raised some funds for the cause. With some help, the NGO got a vehicle enabling rapid action to rescue many other Omars.

Now this act of courage and resilience has snowballed into a massive action. Around 20 such tortured kids are rescued every month. Many people, hitherto having an apparently self-centred outlook have started relooking into the purpose of education as not only a means to bring comfort into their own lives but also unto others and to make this world a more habitable place so that it can be called 'civilized'. Chiro says, "It's time we give back to the society. All these years we have been only taking and exercising our fundamental rights, but now it's time to give back by performing our fundamental duties as diligently as possible. This is imperative for the well-being of the nation."

Chiro is still cycling on, spreading the message and not treating Omar's incident as an isolated one. He shares his eye-opening experience, "It is not always night if you close your eyes – it is darkness all around". He encourages and coaxes others to open their eyes and mind. Omar, of course, is now happy to have an education that gives him back the most coveted thing, not food, but dignity. And what does he pray for? He prays that more people are either animal doctors or think like them so that they can feel the pain of human beings better, since they are able to understand the sufferings of even voiceless animals.

Biographer

Dr. Sujit Nayak, an assistant commissioner in the Department of Animal Husbandry, Dairying & Fisheries, is a childhood school friend of Chiro Priyo Mitra. Being a person concerned with the welfare of animals and poor farmers, he was touched by Chiro's selfless act of humanity and instantly agreed to write this biography.

moJOsh Inspirator Power 6:
The Power of Gratitude

"Gratitude unlocks the fullness of life. It turns what we have into enough, and more. It turns denial into acceptance, chaos to order, confusion to clarity. It can turn a meal into a feast, a house into a home, a stranger into a friend."

~ Melody Beatties

Thought Leadership for Reflection: Most people in the world are not grateful for their life, job, family, home, the body they have, without realizing that many do not have these. Very few even express gratitude for waking up every morning, without realizing that many did not wake up that day. We are not grateful for the little or big things that make our life meaningful, and in the process, we do not understand the attitude of gratitude. And thus we are never happy with what we have. When one is content, one has the integrity to feel the gratitude.

Ideas for Action: Learn to have the integrity to be mindfully grateful for every little thing you have. Remember the old, wise proverb at all times: "I cried because I had no shoes until I met a man who had no feet." Let's be grateful for waking up every day and the energy of your day will change. Let us be grateful for the wonderful world and our beautiful being. Let us be grateful for everything small and big.

7

From Dependent to Dependable: A Model for Change

David Dror

Bimla Devi and I are walking under a scorching sun down the dirt paths of Dialpur, in Vaishali district of Bihar. To our right, an elderly woman squats in the open fields, the folds of her sari the only modesty she can afford. The extreme brightness of the light flattens and dulls the emerald of the fields and the blue of the sky. Only Bimla Devi's turquoise sari, washed so many times that the cotton has turned transparent, shimmers slightly as we walk. Surely, if it were not so hot, we would be trailed by a band of curious children, but they all seem to be hiding in the meagre shade of their homes, one-room structures of mud and straw. They are not the only ones seeking shade: armies of buzzing flies lay in waiting on the piles of cow dung cakes at the front of every home. Bimla Devi is telling me about the day last month when both her daughter and her son were so ill that she absolutely had to take them to see a doctor. "Earlier, if anyone of us got sick," she says, "my heart would shake with fear. What if the doctor wanted some test or some medicine that I just could not afford? What would I do then? Do you know how much money these things cost? I would have been finished!"

But Bimla Devi and thousands of other villagers in India and abroad are no longer afraid of their lives coming to a catastrophic halt every time they or their children fall ill. Because of a programme developed and implemented by Prof. David Dror and his NGO, Micro Insurance Academy (MIA), they are now insured by their villages' not-for-profit health insurance co-operatives. Bimla Devi, who supports her family on an average of ₹100 a day, pays a yearly premium of ₹222 for a policy designed by the villagers themselves. "When the doctor recommended that I should take my child to have a lab exam, I did not even hesitate," she says. "I knew our insurance would pay for it. Can you imagine what a relief that was to me? Can you understand what a relief that is to all the mothers in the village?"

Somewhere behind us, David Dror has stopped for a moment to speak to a group of earnest villagers gathered in front of a small courtyard. They are telling him of a glitch in the policy they have designed, and of a problem with a clinic that is not keeping to the agreed rates.

At 6'2", David literally towers over the villagers now gathered round him in the courtyard on this blistering day in Dialpur. Elegant in his crisp plaid shirt, light-footed in his perfectly polished shoes, David, 72, looks foreign in every way. And yet, he does not seem out of place at all. His body language is comradely, fully engaged. Everyone I talked to during that long day in the village of Vaishali, literate and illiterate alike, knew the details of their insurance plan inside out. They also told me that David is a bit of an enigma in these parts, well-liked and respected, but mysterious nonetheless. "We are grateful to him, of course," they say. But what they have not been able to figure out is this: why would this *firangi*, who has come from a country no one had even heard of, want to do anything for them?

It would be difficult indeed for anyone to grasp the extent of David's devotion: the countless hours spent in the field, the relinquishment of comforts he could have taken for granted, the constant travel on potholed roads, the endless bureaucracy and fundraising, the concentrated troubleshooting. Two years ago, 1,200 people in the district were insured by the mutual insurance co-op which MIA seeded and nurtured into being. By 2015, the co-op boasts of a membership of 5,500. Without the initiative and support of MIA, it would have never happened. Without Prof. David Dror, there would be no MIA.

❧

While Bimla Devi and I speak, her daughter joins us – a slip of a girl with long brown braids; her dress, which used to be pink, is spotless. "How long does it take for the professor to travel from Delhi?" she asks shyly, shifting the weight of her worn backpack, surely heavier than she is. They listen intently as I describe the travel from the mythical city of Delhi to this tiny hamlet in the sun. "I am sure I will never see it", says Bimla Devi, taking her daughter's hand in her own, "but I hope she might, someday".

❧

I first met David Dror during a coffee break at a 'festival of ideas' in the south of India. David, a compatriot, told me of his enterprise, microinsurance. While it was clear that what he was telling me was important, that word he used again and again was so mundane, so lackluster, that I struggled to stay present. Insurance? That same multi-billion dollar industry that has pushed the price of healthcare out of reach? How was this professor, as intelligent and sincere as he might be, going to save India's poor with insurance? I surely was not the first to respond with some incredulity. "Insurance companies have a bad reputation because of their own fault," he responded, "but we are talking about something else, about self-reliance, about taking responsibility for one's future." Then he said something which really caught my attention, "Until the world's poor are able to reduce their extreme vulnerability by banding together, they will never climb out of their hole. The upper classes are never going to do it for them. With our insurance co-ops, we are showing them a way to take back their own power."

David's idea is truly revolutionary, and better yet, it works. At present, some 40,000 people, mostly in India but also in Nepal, and some 1,85,000 in Cambodia, are insured with support from David's initiative; he aims at reaching at least one million people in his own lifetime. David says that all the research (his own often-cited academic work included), has proven that the lack of insurance is one of the main reasons the very poor cannot remedy their situation no matter how hard they try. "Every illness or accident, every crisis, can ruin an entire family's long years of struggle to save and get ahead. A sudden misfortune might cause you or me a challenge of sorts. It might force us to make some kind of sacrifice elsewhere. But for a very poor family," he says, "it would be a total catastrophe. They might be forced to sell their land to pay a hospital bill or the ensuing convalescence, and take loans which might force them into servitude and keep them indentured for life. So why can't the concept of mutual financial guarantee, in other word insurance, be used to help those who are most in need of it? Now all I need is time – and generous grants and support. I must reach my goals while I am still alive," he says, "This is my motto – and this is why I am in a hurry."

As a foreign correspondent based in India, I had, of course, met many people with grand ideas for saving the country and saving her people. But I remembered David Dror's words long after our chance meeting, his quiet yet absolute self-assuredness and obvious devotion to making the world a better place. Eventually, I decided to give him a call and go have a look for myself.

✎

We are on a jeep from Patna, the capital of Bihar, out into the countryside. David is in perpetual motion from country to country, village to village, through underdeveloped regions travelling over difficult roads, visiting government offices, nineteen hours a day, seven days a week. He has returned from Kenya the evening before our trip to Bihar, and on the day following our trip, he will be going to Bangladesh. In between trips, David works from his office in Delhi, a short ride from his modest home. From out the window of our jeep, we observe drivers negotiating traffic jams, we smell the stench of open sewers, and we see beautiful people with friendly, open smiles. The roads look like they have been bombed as a punishment for some crime committed by the population ten generations ago.

"The lives of the people I meet are so hard," David says as we ride. "They are gracious and warm, but this does not change the fact that they are in a long and continual fight for survival. They lack drinking water, toilets, electricity; they are chronically on the brink of disaster. In another roll of the dice," he adds, "it could have been me."

During our trip, David gives an overview of microinsurance, and his baby – MIA. The MIA team brings together the residents of a given village – all belonging to the most underprivileged segments of the population. MIA educates them about the advantages of mutual financial guarantee and the how-tos of forming their own insurance co-op. Next come the many discussions about what the residents of this specific village want and need from their insurance policies. Over the next several months, the villagers engage in a democratic, informed process until finally reaching a consensus. Together, the villagers decide on the premiums, the co-pay, what exactly is to be covered and who will govern their scheme. Eventually, David and the MIA will unite these smaller, village-based insurance co-ops into larger, sturdier entities.

"Insurance companies have a bad reputation because of their own fault. But we are talking about something else, about self-reliance, about taking responsibility for one's future."
~ David Dror

At lunch, in a small, run-down dhaba at the side of the road, we eat piles of fresh rotis with dal and some *ghobi* manchurian. David is friendly with everyone and joins in the laughter but something, and not only his foreign looks, marks him apart. "I mean no insult or disrespect," he says as we continue on our way through the green countryside and the threadbare villages, "but after every trip into the field, I give thanks for my great luck at being born where I was born. I have been awarded the incredible fortune of being in the position of a giver and not in the position of a taker. This knowledge keeps me humble".

꿈

David Dror was born and raised in Jerusalem, to Jewish parents of German birth – intellectual progressives who believed that the purpose of life was to make a better world. David's grandfather, a well-known professor and orientalist from Berlin, had a great influence on his grandson. "He always taught me that the only way to achieve anything was to do it on my own," David recalls. Once, his grandfather asked him if he would like a radio; when the boy answered that he would indeed, the grandfather bought him all of the components with instructions to build one himself. "The other kids made fun of me for my overly serious nature, and for my fastidiousness," he says and recalls another anecdote about his grandfather. "He used to say – do you know how the British Empire was lost? When the last soldier, in the last jungle at the last frontier lost his self-respect and failed to wear his hat or tuck in his shirt."

From the time David finished his studies, he took on positions that gave him the opportunity to work for the betterment of working people's conditions, first in Israel and then in Geneva, where he held senior positions in the International Labor Organization (ILO). His office in those days was so comfortable, facing the famous lake with a view of the Alps. "It was during this time," he recalls, "that I came to a far-reaching conclusion – that the governmental organizations cannot and do not even really want to bring about a truly just social order. That's the truth. I came to understand that the only way forward was through people's *voluntary participation in improving their own lives.* Eventually, I realized that I would have to implement that goal on my own." David developed his model for microinsurance at Erasmus University, Rotterdam, in the Netherlands and started doing fieldwork in rural India in 2005. Five years later, he packed up his bags and moved to Delhi, as far from the Geneva Lake and his fastidious childhood as one could get. "It took some time of course," he says, "but once I became used to the dust and the sweat and the constant stimuli of the senses, I was able to see India and Indians more clearly. And yes, I really like what I see."

⤳

Two hours' drive from the shaky bridge over the Ganges is the green and peaceful Gorigama, completely removed from the buzz and the grime of Patna. Gorigama is a village of practically only women and children; the men work elsewhere, returning seldom, if at all. Most residents have come for the meeting, sitting in a large circle on the ground, on a large blue tarp laid out among the haystacks; the children run about or lie quietly on their mother's laps. David sits right down with them, cross-legged on the blue tarp. The first item on the agenda: the entire group sings a song in honour of David, and then put a garland of marigolds around his neck. The presentation is followed by a circle discussion, led by David (with the help of an interpreter). David asks them very specific questions about the workings of their insurance co-op, set up by MIA three years ago. A woman, uninsured as yet, quietly reveals her hesitations; the other women respond point by point, encouraging her to join.

"Many make the mistake of thinking that the poor and illiterate are hard of understanding," David told me later that evening, over our modest dinner in our modest Patna inn, "but the opposite is true. What they lack is resources, not intelligence. Most of those I meet are bright and clear-headed; they are more able than anyone else to define their own needs."

I find out it is David's birthday, so we raise a toast and share our wishes over lukewarm beer and re-heated *pakora*. He shares stories with me; one is about a woman in the village we had visited that morning. "I met Daulat Devi, together with a 100 other women in saris, seated in the small primary school – really just a room without furniture. Daulat Devi could hardly conceal her two arms, awkwardly immobilized in plaster, inside the folds of her sari. She had broken both arms when she fell during Holi. She went to the hospital, and the consultation, X-ray and treatment fees came to some seem out of place at all ₹1800, by far too large a sum for her to afford. Luckily, she was insured with *Swastya Kamal*, (the name of their community-based insurance) for a yearly premium of ₹521, a small fortune for her that covers her and her family. Because of this coverage, all of her hospital expenses were reimbursed and she was also paid a sum to compensate for the wages lost during her recuperation. She told us she would have had to borrow money from questionable sources, and would have never climbed out of that hole."

MIA educates the villagers about the advantages of mutual financial guarantee and the how-tos of forming their own insurance co-op.

David's work may lack glamour, but he is highly appreciated by his peers and has won many prestigious awards. And yet, year after year, he finds himself, begging bowl in hand, scrambling to collect donations to meet the requirements of his not-for-profit organization, MIA. "It gets easier as our memberships grow and the model proves itself," he adds, "but it is still the most difficult part of my job. Even the Indian government makes life hard and sees no real reason to support our work. They say, 'It is not a free hospital and you are not dispensing free medicine, so why should we support you?' And European philanthropists ask me why I cannot collect from wealthy Indians. How can I explain to them that the Indian upper class, more often than not, is simply not interested in pulling the poor out of poverty?" David explains the current philanthropic model – if the master likes me, he will give me some money; if he doesn't, he will not. "This model is deeply flawed," he says, "how can it be that the real and urgent humanitarian needs of such a large segment of the population depend on the personal tastes of those with money in their pockets?"

For Dror, one cannot count on private money to truly change the world. Sadly, the governments have not been able to, or willing to do this either. "I have come to the conclusion," David says, "that neither of them truly care about the poor population or about allowing these people control over their lives. For them, the poor are mostly a nuisance. What would make governments and the upper classes most happy is if the poor would do everyone a favour and just give up, give in or give way. Besides, there are political entities with a definite interest in keeping the downtrodden down. The poor know all of this very well, believe me. That is why they understand the value of our innovative model; they know, as I do, that no one wants to pay all their bills forever. They accept the tool we give them with grave gratitude – at last, a way to just do it for themselves with dignity and self-respect."

～

I ask David if he feels that it is the poorest population of India that will lead the way forward to better social protection, and his answer is quick and clear, "Rural India is the backbone of responsible India in many ways, and has always been", he says, "it would not be surprising that it should lead the way into a sensible social order as well. This is how it was in Europe of the 19th and early 20th century. The farmers – poor, uneducated, of little interest to the financial sector – led the way in creating mutual aid societies, local savings and loan and local insurance pools. India has banks and many vertical programmes, yet in rural areas, the real power broker remains the money lender, and the government is often viewed as part of the problem, not the solution. In such a scenario, it is the poor who will lead the way forward. By the way, it seems to be the women who get it more than the men do; they have been more abused by the current power system and are more aware of its inherent problems. So accurately speaking, it is the poor women who will lead the way."

On our return to Patna, we sat quietly, checking out the world outside our comfortable, air-conditioned jeep. We passed through a town so tightly packed with people, animals, vehicles and activity that it was impossible to see the road. I watched David watch the people and a thought occurred to me. I asked him if when he looks at them – the couples with their children, vegetable vendors, drivers of bullock carts, teenagers with their arms around each other on their way home from school, old women bent and worn with heavy baskets on their head – he sees only 'insured' and 'non- insured'.

"No," he answers, pausing to think and phrase his answer carefully, "what I see when I look at every person we pass is their human condition. Tomorrow something bad could happen to any one of them, God forbid. But, there is no reason whatsoever that it should destroy their life. When my work succeeds, and it must happen while I am still alive, they will no longer lead a life of continual danger and threat, they will know instead the taste of security. When I look at them, this is what I see."

David, his face alight, turns his gaze back to the awful, wonderful chaos and finally that word, 'insurance', loses its dull grayness and takes on an entirely different meaning.

Biographer

Aimee Ginsburg served as the India Correspondent for *Yedioth Achronoth*, Israel's largest daily newspaper, for 13 years. During her 16 years in India, she appeared often in the electronic media as well as a commentator on Indian affairs and on India-Israel relations. She was a columnist and writer for *Outlook*, *The Times of India* and *Open* magazine. She has also lived closely among the Indian sadhus and rural populations. Currently, she lives and writes in Los Angeles.

moJOsh Inspirator Power 7:
The Power of Creativity

"The desire to create is one of the deepest yearnings of the human soul."

~ Dieter Uchtdorf

Thought Leadership for Reflection: All of us are born with the gift of creativity. We have the power to create our own life, our own world, our own dreams and or own vision. Creativity is a phenomenon whereby we use our imagination to form original ideas and new ways of doing things.

Ideas for Action: Have the integrity to create your own destiny. Be creative to find ways to fulfill your plans in your lifetime. Find creative ways to use the gift of imagination and become the creative force of our own life. You can create a plan for your life, you can create your purpose, your vision, your legacy. You can create change and you have the creation of recreating and renewing yourself every day.

8

Sticking the Neck Out

John Graham

My name is John Graham and since 1983, I've help lead the Giraffe Heroes Project, a global non-profit that moves people to stick their necks out to help solve tough public problems and gives them tools to succeed.

Our strategy is very simple:

We find people already sticking their necks out as agents of change (we call them Giraffe Heroes) and tell their stories in our publications and speeches, on our website, in schools and in traditional and social media. Others see or hear these stories and are inspired to take on the public problems important to *them.*

This simple strategy works. Storytelling really does shift attitudes and move people into action, as it has for thousands of years, in every culture, in every place.

Who are these Giraffe Heroes whose stories we tell? They're men and women, young and old, from every ethnic and economic background, from over 60 countries. They're tackling every kind of public problem, from racism to poverty to violence against women.

They're people like:

Musharraf Hussein is an imam in Nottingham, U.K, and a strong public voice for respectful coexistence among all faiths, and against extremists within Islam who recruit young Muslims to be terrorists. To the extremists, he's a marked man.

Sister Lucy Kurien, in India, is a Giraffe Hero for a lifetime of brave and selfless acts of combating domestic violence prevalent in her society, providing shelters to victims of that violence, and rescuing abandoned women and kids who were or are victims of trafficking.

Charles Jacobs quit his job as a successful management consultant to co-found the American Anti-Slavery Group where he publishes articles, testifies before Congress, develops programmes for schools and leads abolitionist conferences. Thanks to Jacobs and his allies, modern-day slavery is now an issue on the international agenda.

At 15, **Amy Cada's** goal was to prove that young people are a largely untapped but massive resource as volunteers. Now out of college, she's led more successful fundraising campaigns and created more service organizations than most people attempt in a lifetime. These include YouthLead, a campaign to build and support youth-adult partnerships in communities and boardrooms nationwide.

Subhash Chandra Agrawal pushes past innumerable challenges to skillfully use India's Right to Information Act to force better governance in public agencies, advancing the public good.

Through decades of violent turmoil, **Tajwar Kakar** has been fighting for the freedom of Afghanistan and for the rights of its women. He has faced death threats to advocate for the education of young women so they can take part in the rebuilding of their country.

In the past 34 years, we've honoured over 1,300 Giraffe Heroes like the six I mentioned above.

Realizing that inspiration alone often is not enough, we follow up our stories of Giraffe Heroes with speeches, books, blogs, social media posts and trainings in leadership and citizen action. Since 1991, we've been bringing Giraffe civic education programmes to schools and youth organizations all over the world, helping young people build lives as courageous and compassionate citizens.

Our work has always been global, but in 2008 we formed a subsidiary, Giraffe Heroes International (GHI), to launch

Giraffe affiliates that are now present in India, Nepal, Sierra Leone, Kenya, Egypt, Zimbabwe, Singapore and in the Muslim community in the UK. In each place, we set up a local clone of the Giraffe Heroes Project and give speeches, do media interactions, visit schools and conduct training in active citizenship.

In addition to the affiliates, GHI has been engaged in peace-building projects in Sudan, Israel/Palestine and Ukraine. We've stuck our own necks out to train political activists in Egypt and expose what amounts to cultural genocide by the Chinese government in Tibet.

As you might imagine, as often as we can, we ask these Giraffe Heroes why they what they do, why they take these risks and work so hard to help other people? Nobody pays them to do it. Nobody orders them to do it.

Many of them tell us, in so many words, that this is a foolish question. The problem was right in front of them, they'll say, and nobody else was acting – so what else were they supposed to do?

The more you talk to them, the clearer it gets that Giraffe Heroes are motivated by a strong sense that what they're doing is meaningful to them – that is, it satisfies a personal sense of purpose at the core of their being.

The more you talk to them, the clearer it gets that Giraffe Heroes are motivated by a strong sense that what they're doing is *meaningful* to them – that is, it satisfies a personal sense of purpose at the core of their being.

It's this deep conviction that then drives them forward. It's what makes them so effective in solving problems, and so inspiring to people who hear their stories.

Their source of motivation is not surprising.

Philosophers and spiritual leaders have been telling us for millennia that there's no deeper human need and no more powerful yearning than to live a life we know is meaningful.

We all want to be able to look at ourselves in the mirror and know that what we're doing counts, that we're not just on this planet to take up space.

Look at your own experiences, dear reader–at home, at work, in the community. Like Giraffe Heroes, you may work very hard and there may be trials, but when you're doing something you know is meaningful to you, there's also energy, an excitement, a deep satisfaction of being in the right place at the right time. You're more inspiring to others, and they're attracted to join you, to follow your lead.

And you're much more likely to get the results you want.

Have you felt this? Do you know what I'm talking about?

If meaning is this important, it's fair to ask – where does meaning come from?

We ask the Giraffe Heroes the same question; they should know. Their answer, almost universally, is that the most stable, long-term source of meaning in their lives is service – helping solve tough public problems, making life better for other people.

I confess, this is not a lesson I learned as a young man. I thought I knew then what made my life meaningful and it wasn't service. It was an adventure: the bigger and more dangerous the adventure, the better.

I went to sea on a freighter when I was 17. This was, mind you, way before container ships. Cargo vessels then had crews of 50 or 60 really tough seamen, all of whom were determined to teach me lessons they knew I would never get in school. I leave the detailed stories for another day except to say that the first port of call ended with a pitched brawl with local stevedores and a hangover that lasted three days.

But I came back changed, and it was by more than a barroom brawl. Roaming around the Far East as a 17-year-old opened me to a vision of a wider world, pulsing with energy, colours and excitement. I wanted more.

I spent the summer after my sophomore year in college hitchhiking in Europe and North Africa. I walked into Algeria just one week after the ceasefire had supposedly ended a brutal war there. The situation was very fragile. I wore a US flag across my chest: the message was, "Don't shoot me; I'm not French." It worked – rebel patrols stopped cars going in my direction and told the drivers to take me where I wanted to go.

The next summer, 1963, I was part of the first direct ascent of the North Wall of Mt. McKinley, the highest peak in North America–a climb so dangerous nobody's done it since.

I kept upping the ante. After college, I hitchhiked around the world. I got a press pass from the *Boston Globe* and covered every war I found along the way – in Cyprus, Eritrea, Laos and Vietnam.

So by the age of 22, I had gained the following perspective on life:

1. There was a huge wonderful, exciting world out there.
2. Nothing mattered but physical adventure, the bigger and riskier the better.
3. I was indestructible. None of my adventures would ever do me in.

To say that this perspective was shallow would be generous. But I gained a lesson from those early experiences I've lived by ever since. That lesson is that a full life invites passionate involvement, and that sometimes means taking risks. However, this lesson needed to be tempered with another lesson, one I didn't get until much later.

The second lesson was this: what's important is not the risks, what's important is knowing what to take risks *for*. The most significant risks often challenge not the body but the soul. They're about finding what makes our lives truly meaningful and then going for it with everything we have.

As I said, this second lesson was lost on me as a young man. The risks I took then were all physical. I did what I did because of the adrenaline buzz.

After that year spent hitchhiking around the world, I was faced with a challenge. How could I earn a living and still lead an adventurous life? I joined the US Foreign Service. It didn't disappoint. I soon found myself in the middle of the first revolution in Libya, and then the war in Vietnam. But I was no patriot. My motivation was still adventure... and power. Doing well in dangerous assignments was pushing me quickly up the State Department's promotion ladder.

After Vietnam, the department sent me to Stanford for a year and for most of that year I would walk on the shadowed sides of the streets in Palo Alto, California, to avoid sniper fire. The promotions kept coming. But what I was doing and why began to sit in my stomach like a bad meal. You see, mixed in with all these adventures, all the 'tough guy stuff' I was doing was a set of ideals – about peace, about fairness in the world, about ending the suffering caused by wars and revolutions and poverty. It was a small, nagging voice from my heart and I ignored it for many years.

The only mistake you can make is to ignore the quest, to live and die without having made a difference.

Then came a turning point.

In 1977, I was transferred to the US Mission to the United Nations as an assistant to Ambassador Andrew Young. Part of my job there was to represent the United States on the Security Council Committee that dealt with South Africa and apartheid, which, as you know, was a racist system subjugating blacks. The UN was supposed to enforce an arms embargo on South Africa. It had been imposed because guns sold to the South African government in those years were used to enforce apartheid, to kill blacks. But the embargo leaked like a sieve. Why? Because there were huge amounts of money involved in the arms trade, and the arms dealers had their friends in parliaments in Europe and in the US Congress.

I ignored my instructions to not make waves and instead worked secretly for months to tighten that embargo. I did that by helping the Third World countries increase their pressure against my own government. Once our Secretary of State received a strong message from an African foreign minister complaining about American hypocrisy in not enforcing the arms embargo. In it, I recognized words that I myself had drafted two weeks before.

Then I went to my bosses and remarked on the huge upsurge of pressure coming from the Third World to tighten the embargo, and the enormous pressure being put on the US government to live up to its promises –pressure that I myself had helped generate. It worked. The US agreed to a really tough embargo and the Europeans had no choice but to follow suit. On May 2, 1980, the Security Council passed that embargo and, in time, it helped end apartheid.

At any time in this process, I could have been fired. So why did I do this? Why did I take these risks?

I did it because of that one day spent in South Africa. The day began in the squalor and oppression of the black township of Soweto. I walked down garbage-strewn streets. I felt the hate-filled eyes of hundreds of young black men boring into the back of my white head. I could not blame them. The day ended with a diplomatic cocktail party in Johannesburg's fanciest white suburb, in a mansion surrounded by iron fences and guard dogs.

Apartheid stank and I resolved to do something to end it.

At a deeper level, I took those risks because helping end the injustice of apartheid meant something to me at the deepest place in my soul, something more than adventure or power. It was, however, not lost on me that I had just had the best adventure of my life and it had nothing to do with dodging bullets or hanging off a cliff by a rope.

The experience was like learning to swim.

I couldn't forget what I'd done.

I couldn't forget how to do it.

I couldn't forget the joy and fulfillment I felt in making a difference like that.

I'd found the meaning of my life and, like Giraffe Heroes, I'd found it in service, in bettering the lives of others, in helping solve a significant public problem.

And I am hardly alone.

Since then, I've watched many other people make the same discovery, find the meaning of their lives in service. I've watched them use that discovery to fuel their commitment and energy to take on tough tasks and succeed – and to experience the satisfaction of living their lives to the fullest.

What's been true for them and for me and for the Giraffe Heroes is, or will be, true for you, dear reader. I guarantee it. A year after my experience with the arms embargo, I quit the Foreign Service, because by then I was marching to a different drummer. I wanted to change the world.

I wish I could tell you that it was all a steady upward course from there. But it wasn't. The fact was, I lost my nerve. When I sent my resignation to the State Department, I really hadn't done any financial planning. No sooner had I sent that resignation, I began to panic about money. So, I shelved my plans for saving the world at least for a while and found a job lecturing on cruise ships. I mean, how bad is that?

Well, actually, pretty bad.

My first ship burned and sank in the Gulf of Alaska, leaving me and seven other men lost in a lifeboat in a typhoon, 140 miles from land. After 12 hours, we were all dying of the cold. 530 other passengers and crew had already been rescued, but with the winds now blowing at 65 knots and the sea at 30 feet, it would have been suicidal for the helicopters to come back. Our fate rested on a coast guard ship frantically searching for us in the storm. It would be dark in half an hour. Visibility in that storm was perhaps 50 yards. The odds of that ship finding us even in daylight were very slim and they could never find us in the dark. The lifeboat was taking on water. An icy rain beat down on us like bullets. We would be dead by morning.

It seemed pretty clear that, after all my near misses, that time I really was going to die. There is a long story behind this, but let me just give you the bottom line. I was not a religious person but believe me, in a situation like that, one is led to pray. But my 'prayer' soon turned into an angry rant. Why was I being wiped out like this? After I'd helped end apartheid. After I'd left the foreign service to make the world a better place. I was leaning into this new life. Now I was being wiped out? I deserved an explanation! So I screamed into the storm, WHY?

I don't think the other seven heard anything, but for me, a voice boomed out of the storm: "Don't kid yourself," the voice said in so many words. "You've found the meaning of your life in service, but because you're worried about money, now you're running away from what you know brings meaning to your life. If you keep running, you might as well die out here, which will happen very soon. You have to make a decision: will you commit to a life of service—or die out here in the storm?"

I was freezing to death. I had no resistance left. I just looked up into the teeth of the storm and mumbled, "Yes."

I know this sounds like a B-grade movie, but in that instant, an instant of surrender, the coast guard cutter *Boutwell* burst out of the storm, heading so right for us that, had the lookout not spotted us, it might have cut our lifeboat in two. The sailors tossed us a rope and with frozen hands, I managed to tie it to a cleat near the port bow. The next big wave ripped not just the cleat but the whole top board off and the lifeboat began to founder. So coast guard men in wetsuits jumped aboard and, one by one, we were hoisted to safety.

I kept the promise I made in that lifeboat.

I returned to New York. I met Ann Medlock who had just started the Giraffe Heroes Project. And you know the story from there.

I think that this experience on the cruise ship happened to me because of the extraordinary efforts I was making to run away from what I knew would make my life meaningful. In running away, I was devaluing my life.

Of course, this story is exotic. But I don't think the lesson applies just to me. It's not likely, dear reader that you'll be fighting for your life in a typhoon in the North Pacific, but we are all tested by crises large and small.

Don't make the mistake that I made. Don't ignore the importance of meaning in your life and the role that service plays in providing it. The only mistake you can make is to ignore the quest, to live and die without each one having made a difference.

How can you serve? Where do you start? I don't know what it would be for you. There are plenty of problems out there.

I do know this: each of us has, and will have, unique opportunities to make a difference. A successful life is about spotting those opportunities and acting on them.

I'm not suggesting you quit your day jobs. You can find plenty of ways to make a difference in business, in the government, in the professions and the arts, and certainly, as a citizen.

But I am suggesting that power, money and prestige are no more stable, long-term sources of meaning than was my adventuring. They are tools to help you find and carry out the deeper meanings of your lives–to use your time, energy, contacts and resources to be of service, to help solve tough public problems, to make life better for other people.

The poet Mary Oliver puts it this way: "Tell me, what is it you plan to do with your one and precious life?"

What a question!

It may be the most important question any of us will ever ask. Never give up the search for meaning in your life and never settle for anything less. Find the challenge or problem that you care about, that one with your name on it. Then take it on.

"Tell me, what is it you plan to do with your one wild and precious life?"

Biographer

David Allen is a writer, city planner and manager now living in La Connor, Washington, USA.

moJOsh Inspirator Power 8:
The Power of Curiosity

"I have no special talents; I am just very curious."
~ Albert Einstein

Thought Leadership for Reflection: Curiosity means a strong desire to know or learn something. Very few people have a penchant for continuous improvement and growth through learning. Most feel they know enough, without realizing they know nothing. Curiosity is our birth gift to learn more and grow more. If we are not curious, we stop learning.

Ideas for action: Your integrity to know more about yourself and to be socially conscious will unlock your curiosity. Learn to enquire about things you don't know or understand. Learn to ask questions and seek answers to enhance your learning. Remember, your future belongs to you and the future overall belongs to people who are curious to explore new ideas, to challenge dogmas, to question and poke at the old ways of thinking to create significant new breakthroughs.

9

For the Love of the Wild

K. M. Chinnappa

Hunting was a way of life in the verdant forests and foothills of the Western Ghats in Karnataka's Coorg district. It was an integral part of the Coorgi tradition, folklore, manhood, sports, food and commerce. From poor, forest-dwelling tribesmen to the flamboyant royalty and courtiers in bustling Mysore, everyone loved hunting. But one man stood tall to end this way of life – K. M. Chinnappa.

Chinnappa was born in 1941 in Kumtur village near Nagarhole. His father was a soldier who fought in the World War I. Chinnappa spent his youth roaming the forests of his ancestral land, listening to birds, watching the cavalcade of animals in their habitat, absorbing the everyday miracles of the rich ecosystem. An enduring love for nature was thus born in him. Like his father, he, too, would become a mustachioed soldier, but with a difference. He would become a gun-toting, frontline warrior of the forests, dedicated to protecting wildlife. In Chinnappa's own words, "Wildlife is the purpose of my life."

In 1967, Chinappa joined the Nagarhole National Park as a forester. The park was in ruins. Hunting had taken its toll. There were hardly any deer left, forget tigers and other big game. To cultivate rice, villagers had encroached on the swamps – the beloved playground of the elephants. Tribesmen lived in clusters deep within the park to collect forest produce, ranging from honey to berries. Livestock herders grazed their cattle on the park's grasslands. Hunters preyed on animals and birds. Poachers preyed on tigers for their skin and elephants for their tusks. Timber mafia thrived. Sandalwood smugglers roamed with abandon. The destroyers of Nagarhole's environment employed a range of weapons – hunters used shotguns, tribesmen used snares and livestock herders used poison. Wildlife protection laws were weak and the forest department concentrated on logging, misguidedly uprooting the diversity of natural vegetation to replace them with the monocultures of teak. "If this devastation had continued, I was dead certain that there would have been no wildlife left in Nagarhole in 30 years," rued Chinnappa.

Chinappa became a one-man army to reverse this process, and he succeeded. In less than a quarter of a century, Nagarhole revived, expanding from 250 square kilometres to 640 square kilometres. The poachers have retreated, the encroachers now gone and the hunters are virtually extinct, restoring Nagarhole to its rightful inhabitants – tigers, panthers, leopards, sloth bears, jackals, wild boars, porcupines, hares, langur and varieties of deer. In the bad old days, tigers had to roam 200 square kilometres before they could find prey. Now they can find it within 12 square kilometres. The elephants are back where they belonged – in the lush swamps and bamboo groves. What was the trick behind this success? Chinnappa explains, "All you have to do is, stop human interference. Just leave the forests alone and they will regenerate themselves."

> *"All you have to do is, stop human interference. Just leave the forests alone and they will regenerate themselves."*
> ~ K.M. Chinnappa

Chinnappa was the right man at the right time. In 1972, coaxed by several leading Indian conservationists, the then Prime Minister Indira Gandhi took a slew of measures to protect the environment. Several laws were enacted and sanctuaries in Kanha, Corbett, Ranthambore, Bandipur and Nagarhole among others were pulled back from the brink of destruction. Forest departments had new directions, muscle and teeth. Still, keeping the humans out of the forests was not easy. Chinnappa paid a high personal price to fulfill his mission and safeguard Nagarhole – he was arrested, jailed, transferred, his home was burned down. But he has no regrets. "What's the use of just going to the office? I led a colourful life," says Chinnappa with his characteristic optimism.

To protect the wildlife, Chinnappa had to take on a range of human beings who lived on the wild side of life. He captured a number of poachers and smugglers, and filed court cases against them. But they were all acquitted in no time and were back to their wicked ways. He realized he would have to terrorize them, make it really dangerous for them to hunt and poach. He took up the gun and did not hesitate to shoot. He recalls, "Nobody used high-calibre guns. I had only a 12-bore rifle, and I used only buckshot. But at that time, it was enough." He remembers the legend of a tribesman whom the locals nicknamed Parari Thimma – Vanishing Thimma. He was a notorious poacher who nimbly eluded forest guards. Chinnappa began tracking him and one day, shot at him. And then he vanished forever! Chinnappa became the local legend. Supporters hailed him as a hero, the Phantom of the jungles. Poachers called him 'the devil' who stalked their hunting grounds. Chinnappa used his immense knowledge of forest trails, tracking spoor, jungle craft, fabled night vision and stealth maneuvers to ambush poachers and hunters. Guided by moonlight, he silently crept upon the forest brigands and opened fire. It marked the end of the old way of life in Nagarhole.

But nothing happened without resistance. In no time, the threatened "vested interests" – profiteering poachers, unscrupulous smugglers, wealthy hunters, criminals, mafia operators and politicians – ganged up against Chinnappa. Even the villagers rose in revolt. For Chinnappa, life took a curious turn. On the one hand, the regeneration of Nagarhole won high praise. He bagged the Karnataka Chief

Minister's Gold Medal in 1983, received an award from the Wildlife Conservation Society and foreign environmentalists showered him with glowing tributes in books and magazines. His Spartan way of life, incorruptibility and military discipline became legendary. Ullas Karanth, a leading wildlife biologist, says, "Chinnappa is a man of integrity. He is tough, efficient and incredibly courageous in the face of grave physical danger. His accomplishments in Nagarhole are undoubtedly a major milestone in the history of Indian wildlife conservation." His peers admired and respected him. But some of the locals feared and hated him. In 1988, one of Chinnappa's guards publicly shot a local coffee planter who had killed and eaten his pet samba deer. The dispute spun out of control and soon, local poachers instigated a public agitation, accusing Chinnappa of masterminding the murder. Bowing to political pressure, Chinnappa was arrested and jailed for 12 days. Eventually, he was cleared of all charges and reinstated.

But groups with vested interests continued to persecute him. He was implicated in the killing of a poacher in 1992 and a riot erupted. A frenzied mob ransacked the forest department's buildings, burnt vehicles, assaulted staff, set fire to large swathes of forest land and set ablaze Chinnappa's ancestral home. Once again, he was cleared of all charges, but this time, Chinnappa decided to call it quits. He could understand why the poachers, smugglers and politicians ganged up against him. But the fact that they could enlist the support of the villagers had a profound impact on him. He realized that he needed to move to another plane of conservation: education. He had to make the locals realize the practical and moral imperative to protect their environment. Forest protection was not merely the job of foresters. It was a collective responsibility.

And so in 1993, he retired prematurely from the department and started his NGO, the Nagarhole Wildlife Conservation Education Project, to educate the local people, especially the children, about the need to protect the environment. His motto was simple: "Without humans, the forest will flourish. Without forests, we humans cannot flourish." Through forest camps, discussions and slide shows, he opens the doors to a magical kingdom of flora and fauna, encouraging children to take delight in observing nature instead of hunting animals.

His mission also involves fighting legal cases. As the president of Bangalore-based NGO, Wildlife First, Chinnappa and a group of conservationists documented the ecological devastation caused by the iron ore mine operators in Kudremukh. In retaliation, they were slapped with 12 criminal cases. Bittu Sehgal, Editor of the environment magazine *Sanctuary*, says, "Law suits are filed by those who have money or power on their side to prevent public-minded citizens from 'interfering'." The cases dragged on for years and wound up in the Supreme Court, which ordered the closure of the mines in December 2005.

Through all his trials and tribulations, one thing remained undiminished – his sheer will to save the forests.

Chinnappa's accomplishments are all the more laudable because they were won against the stiffest odds. He endured setbacks, difficulties, threats, attacks, vilification, arrests and court cases. But, remarkably, he has emerged unscathed; his innocence, courage, dedication, honour and optimism intact. He is completely devoid of bitterness. He chooses to forget the troublemakers who made life so difficult for him and his loyal wife Radha, but remembers fondly the senior officers and lowly guards who stood by him. Through all his trials and tribulations, one thing remained undiminished – his sheer will to save the forests. With deep conviction, he says, "If you have the will, you can do wonders."

Today, Chinnappa derives enormous satisfaction from the guns – the yesteryear symbol of manhood – that lie rusting in many a Coorgi home. Cheering the end of that bygone era are the sights and sounds of a promising new life, symbolized by the swaying foliage and barking deer.

Biographer

Anita Pratap is a Karamveer Puraskaar award recipient, and is an expatriate Indian writer and journalist. In 1983, she was the first journalist who interviewed LTTE chief V. Prabhakaran. She won the George Polk Award for television reporting of the takeover of Kabul by the Taliban. She was also the India bureau chief of CNN.

moJOsh Inspirator Power 9:
The Power of Loving to Learn

"I don't love studying. I hate studying, I love learning. Learning is beautiful."

~ Natalie Portman

Thought Leadership for Reflection: Loving the process of learning is one the of the life's most important skills. Most people in the world have never developed this skill. For them, learning is drudgery or studying to pass a test or earn a degree. This power has two aspects: one is attitude and the other is learning to actually enjoy the work behind the process.

Ideas for action: Keep an open mind and have the integrity to learn in every moment; be it while reading a book, watching a movie, having a conversation with a friend, cycling by the bay or just spending time with yourself, every moment is loaded with learning, provided you are mindful and have the love of learning from every little situation and moment.

10

Good to Great

Karan Paul

"If life is a test, then time surely is its greatest judge. Time destroys the strongest monuments and extinguishes the brightest of stars. Only the sturdiest foundations and the greatest values pass the trials and tribulations of time."

It was hardly a surprise that Karan Paul began his organization's centenary celebrations address on April 1, 2011, on this philosophical note. A Brown University alumnus, Karan had studied philosophy and literature as an undergraduate. The course of his studies changed when his father died in a tragic terrorist attack in politically charged Assam, where his family owned 50,000 acres of tea plantations. He finally majored in politics. Although dry, the subject helped him understand events, specifically the one that had killed his father. He returned to India to take charge of the family business – Apeejay Surrendra Group.

On April 1, 2011, when Karan addressed the gathering at the centenary celebrations, he said, "As Chairman, it fills me with great pride to stand in front of you as the flame-bearer of the group. It fills me with even greater pride to say that those who lit the flame and carried it before me were better men than I: Aminchand, Pyarelal, Jit, Surrendra…"

Hundreds of guests had smiled affectionately and applauded. They knew that the legacy that flowed in Karan's veins had formed the ethos of everything he did. He brought something extra to the table, never took away and always made the pie bigger, just like his father Surrendra had taught him. He had imbibed the sense of purpose of his uncle Jit well and like him, Karan was strong, humble, true, generous and always the best that he could be. He was joyous like his father and believed that happiness was not achieved by more money, more power or more fame, but by building positive relationships with those around him. The sheer presence of formidable names from the industry in the room, listening to him deliver his speech in 2011, was a testament to the fact that to every business partnership and friendship, he had invested something that could not be quantified, something unique that made him who he was. He had lived up to his family legacy of making everyone prosper together – be it business partners or employees. Those present did not completely agree that his forefathers were better men than him. They had grown to love and respect Karan as much as his forefathers. They knew however that he meant every word of what he said.

What nobody there knew was how much time he had spent on choosing every word in his carefully written speech. But his team knew. Their chairman was a tough man to please. Writing his public addresses for him was a task, and given a choice, they'd rather not do it. While they had got better at it over the years, the words they crafted for him were never good enough for their boss, who, among them, they had declared as a writer in disguise!

It wasn't far from the truth actually. Karan had been reading serious literature from a very young age as he finished his schooling between Delhi's Modern High and Kolkata's La Martiniere.

Intellectually and philosophically, business to Karan is his 'good karmic action'. Personally, he believes in the philosophy that one should not steal, cheat or lie. When extrapolated to Karan the businessman, it translates into his companies behaving ethically as they compete hard in a marketplace that often throws up ethical dilemmas. Under his leadership, the Apeejay Group has made substantial business investments and expanded across various business verticals, especially its core businesses of shipping and hotels. As he goes about looking after the strategic growth of his businesses, Karan's ability to create relationships, nurture partnerships and live up to his customer's trust are clearly evident.

Karan's first business as an entrepreneur was a finance and a stock broking company. He ran those businesses for about ten years and sold them in 2006-07. So at the age of 35, Karan had created, run and sold two businesses, exposing him to the complete business cycle, from inception to achieving a profitable sale. The partners he chose to hive off the companies, too, were renowned in their fields, who would invest and grow the two companies as well as bring value to the customers, whose trust these two businesses and Karan had enjoyed tremendously since inception. In keeping 'good company' in his choice of partners, Karan had underlined his personal philosophy that while wealth creation was important, it was not his only goal in business. His forefathers were influenced by Mahatma Gandhi's idea of trusteeship. Karan takes his responsibility to Apeejay's legacy and its stakeholders as something that extends well beyond just creating wealth, and subscribes to the Hindu thought that whatever wealth one accumulates out of desires becomes a part of one's karmic burden, and that wealth can also be an opportunity for those who want to serve.

In keeping 'good company' in his choice of partners, Karan had underlined his personal philosophy that while wealth creation was important, it was not his only goal in business.

Karan had begun to grapple with questions about wealth even as a teenager. Growing up, he felt obligated to work amidst the underprivileged, something he could not do as tragic events overtook his plan. Money, he says, is ephemeral, and acquiring it is not his goal in business; his real purpose is to do the business well. When he took his place in Apeejay, his own personality traits led him to directing the community programmes with a much deeper insight than any other fresh graduate. The first visible community project with Karan's stamp on it began to take shape around 1999, after he interviewed brilliant Indian students, hopeful for admission in his alma mater, Brown University, but without the financial means to do so. In the belief that it was the quality of the mind that makes future leaders, Karan created The Paul Foundation and scholarships were instituted to develop the potential among the young and talented in India. Through scholarships that enable young people with potential to travel in search of knowledge, this foundation opened up new vistas of the mind. In 2009, it took on the challenge of sending slum children around Park Street back to school.

Keeping an ear to the ground helped him create additional lines of remedial support for children who were put back into school but were again in the danger of dropping out.

The Anand Paul Education Support Programme was instituted in 2010 to invest in creating a future for these children with a new approach. Under this programme, education centres were opened in local club rooms and community halls through NGOs who were to identify children who had either dropped out of school or were not enrolled in school, and help them return to school. Karan visited the centres himself during the programme's design stage to gauge if the new approach would be effective and useful. Keeping an ear to the ground helped him create additional lines of remedial support for children who were put back into school but were again in the danger of dropping out; to tackle the parents' tendency to divert the children's attention to other tasks by engaging them in adult literacy and skill training programmes.

Inclusiveness for disabled people, underprivileged children and women is something that Karan often lamented about. He planned a Social Sector Initiatives programme that helped such individuals in a fresh new way to take pleasure in their ability and existence and realize their potential. Karan's objective was to help people with physical disabilities to feel included, independent and empowered against social isolation, marginalization, prejudice, pity and physical challenges like negotiating obstacles in the natural environment. Thus the projects for the disabled went beyond the traditionally held views of charity and welfare, and encompassed rehabilitation, assistive technology, employment, training and recreation. The projects embraced new ways of actualizing productivity and empowerment for the disabled.

In creating programmes for women, Karan's focus was on those suffering, abandoned and battered. Thus, the programmes saw the creation of halfway houses for the mentally challenged and geared to empower them with economic freedom. The children's projects were designed towards the well-being of underprivileged children and their families in order to build ability in them to participate in and benefit from their societies. Research and brainstorming sessions were held with experts so that leaders of the Social Sector Initiatives projects could concentrate on real issues. Partners were chosen carefully with due diligence and Karan constantly urged the team to keep scale, impact and ripple effect in mind as part of programme's design and strategy.

To focus on his own and everybody's efforts, to encourage transparency and ease for those who wanted to reach out to the various welfare trusts of Apeejay for support, Karan ensured that all of his companies documented their community work and processes. In 2006-07, Apeejay's first corporate social responsibility report was published on the corporate website titled 'Living Responsibly'. In Karan's own words from the report, "I know that we can do much more and our efforts seem just drops in the ocean. It is my endeavour and commitment as Chairman of Apeejay Surrendra to allocate more resources and take up projects focused on things that we find meaningful and have a lasting impact." The same focus on what requires urgent effort was seen a few years later, in 2015. Two of the group's companies became the first few to align their corporate social responsibility (CSR) policies with the United Nation's Sustainable Development Goals, under discussion then. A sustainability and social responsibility framework was adopted by Apeejay Tea; it outlined the companies target to protect, conserve and preserve ecosystems and all natural resources in the plantations. A similar framework was adopted by Apeejay Shipping, outlining its target to continuously improve existing systems and processes to minimize pollution or contamination of all natural resources, including marine resources. The Sustainable Development Goals came into effect on January 1, 2016 and the United Nations' 193 member states adopted them as their new Sustainable Development Agenda.

Karan leads a top team of 15 people who represent the various businesses, some of which Karan had inherited when he joined the business as a fresh graduate. Due to his management style, they as well as the mid-level members demonstrated a remarkable rise in team effectiveness, alignment on strategic direction, quality of execution and ability to change. An employee working with his uncle Jit on the restoration of Park Mansions, a heritage property owned by the group, remembers meeting Karan when he took charge of his uncle's dream project, and the meticulous detailing that followed. The result was the coveted Heritage Award which was bestowed upon the building by the Kolkata Municipal Corporation (KMC) and Indian National Trust for Art and Cultural Heritage (INTACH) in 2013. On the other end of the spectrum, Karan has steered the group's FMCG brand, Typhoo Tea, towards launching the first globally certified environmentally sustainable teas to be marketed pan India, with a distinct seal of The Rainforest Alliance certification seal on product packs. The seal is an assurance to customers that the product is sourced from certified farms that adhere to very stringent sustainable agriculture standards that protect environment, biodiversity, waterways, wildlife habitats and the rights and well-being of workers and their families.

Responsible food marketing in India is an important agenda for Karan, after working for many years now making his tea plantations rigorously implement global Sustainable Agricultural Network (SAN) standards. Not only did this launch leapfrog Rainforest Alliance's sustainability campaign in India but also sparked an important debate on the connection between climate change, community, consumption and consumers.

Strong governance around project selection and funding overseen by him directly have ensured that Apeejay has never 'thrown money' on an issue. A large chunk of philanthropic giving continues traditionally, but substantial portions of the funds go into projects that are critical to the causes Karan and his family believe need to be addressed.

A few years ago, Karan invited Pratham Council for Vulnerable Children, a wing of Pratham Mumbai Education Initiative, to study the functioning of Apeejay Schools in his tea plantations in Assam run by the estate management. The objective was to profile the children that study in these schools, review the quality outcomes of the intervention in the schools and suggest intervention plans to make them into 'model schools'.

The Individual Social Responsibility TM (ISRTM), the group's employee volunteering programme initiated in 2007-08, was started after an employee survey and was an extension of what Karan believed in. He was working directly with NGOs and the group's community leaders on project design, field visits, reviewing incremental needs and measuring impact. He thus took ownership of the cause he believed in, be it helping battered women or disabled people or underprivileged children. With ISR™ he offered the same to all his employees. Should they choose to and want to do so, Apeejay employees have the opportunity to take ownership of social causes they believed in and Apeejay lets them do social work in office hours during the working week. The idea Karan was driving at in 2007-08 was very powerful – corporates have different kinds of capital available to them, not just CSR capital and philanthropic capital, but human capital or managerial resources capital. With ISR™, he brought Apeejay's human capital to the forefront.

Karan has tried to create a market of unique reward and recognition; recognition for children who show enterprise in the face of adversity and disability, and for individuals who bring all kinds of value – not just financial – to the society. The Surrendra Paul Memorial Award for Courage honours students who have faced challenges head-on and won. The Anand Paul Memorial Award for Social Service honours schools that are deeply committed to making a difference in society. Non-competitive in spirit, both the awards have been instituted to recognize the contribution of education institutions and young people every year. Apeejay India Volunteer Award, a pioneering national award, was instituted for individual volunteers, corporates with best employee volunteering policy and NGOs with best volunteer engagement policies. This was instituted in 2011 to celebrate volunteering amongst Indians and bring it to the mainstream. Karmaveer Chakra – bronze, silver and gold – are given annually under Apeejay Karmayuga, a character building movement that seeks to inspire Indians towards delivering fundamental duties as enshrined in the Indian constitution and karma as enshrined in India's oldest religious scriptures.

A reward and recognition platform with UK's national charity, the English Federation of Disability Sport (EFDS), created a couple of years back, has ensured that more disabled athletes have access to local competitions. It was the third time that Karan had backed the charity's work after sponsoring the Typhoo Sports for All project in 2009 and

2010 that funded free Disability Inclusion Training across the UK. More than 1,000 disabled athletes were part of the regional qualifiers that lead to the National Junior Athletics Championships climax in June 2015. Over 250 teenagers between ages 12 and 20 took part at Warwick Athletics Stadium. The stadium had a full Track and Field programme on offer, which meant that athletes with a wide range of impairments could take part. This hadn't been possible in many other events.

In each of these projects, Karan has brought the values of integrity, discipline, hard work and innovation. This approach has had many remarkable outcomes. One of the most recent is the celebration of Apeejay's 100-year-milestone as a successful business house with the initiative to undertake 100 community projects. In essence, while Karan was addressing his guests on April 1, 2011, he was implementing the real celebration of the centennial. It's no surprise that he was planning both celebrations at the same time – one unique, meaningful with lasting impact and the second, fun, celebrating relationships, partnerships and friendships.

Strong governance around project selection and funding overseen by Karan directly have ensured that Apeejay has never 'thrown money' on an issue.

In April 2016, Karan committed his fleet of ships and people to being vigilant and to use their information networks globally to break the supply chain of illegal commercial trade in wildlife and animal products. The group's shipping company joined the fight to shut down illegal wildlife trafficking and signed the Buckingham Palace Declaration led by the Duke of Cambridge. Employee training in wildlife protection and illegal wildlife trade began immediately and they quickly aligned with their chairman on an issue that is a direct threat to species and goes against the stability and diversity of our biosphere.

Far away in Assam, another unique project has been underway for more than a year. Karan had drawn up a three-year exhaustive management strategy that saw the group's tea plantations company invest in reducing the impact of human-elephant conflict in Assam. The project was implemented in partnership with the Worldwide Fund for Nature (WWF). Under the programme, new paths that elephants establish to move away from forest areas will be mapped. The tracking start point will be an Apeejay tea garden, thus serving as an early warning to the region of elephants on the move. The route that the elephants take through the group's plantation would be formalized as a movement corridor and hedged by a bio-fence. This will be the first time that bio-fencing (as against electric fencing) will be used as protection that is safe for elephants and other wildlife, with nurseries for growing the thorny bamboo for the bio-fence inside the Apeejay tea estates. A matrix is being developed for the first time to calculate the quantum of loss that is usually borne by the tea estates on account of damage to property, including tea bushes, shade trees and infrastructure, loss of man hours in conflict management and injuries among residents due to the conflict with elephants, who see the estates as an extension of their habitat.

Today, the deaths and injuries to the residents of Apeejay's plantations are already down to nearly nil, even though elephant raids are up exponentially. WWF is certain that the project will be able to decrease human and elephant mortality levels substantially from those recorded in 2013 in Assam tea plantations.

If there is an irony here, it doesn't occur to Karan at all. In life you can either be a passenger or a pilot, it's a choice. Karan has chosen to be a pilot. While he came into business because of inheritance, staying in business has been his own choice and his own drive to succeed – a drive to make something positive of what he had got in his legacy; a drive to self-fulfillment, self-achievement and self-actualization.

Karan works hard at it every day. He laughs when you point that out to him. Perhaps the laughter means that he agrees, or perhaps he laughs because he regularly shrugs off praise, it's difficult to tell. But it is the same hearty laughter of his father, Surrendra, which resonated in Apeejay House in the 1980s, spreading joy. And that, for now, is good enough; good enough for everyone who loves that the simple and humble Karan Paul is in charge of Apeejay's legacy and future.

Biographer

Renu Kakkar is Director, Corporate Social Responsibility and Communications, Apeejay Surrendra Group. Renu joined the group in 2000 and has worked with Karan Paul in various roles across financial services, the Internet and e-commerce, information technology, brand and corporate identity and corporate communications. She is a former journalist with *The Telegraph* and *The Indian Express,* and is an alumnus of Lady Sri Ram College and Indian Institute of Mass Communication, New Delhi.

moJOsh Inspirator Power 10:
The Power of Bravery

"I learned that bravery is not the absence of fear, but the triumph over it. The brave man is not he who does not feel afraid, but he who conquers those fears."

~ Nelson Mandela

Thought Leadership for Reflection: Bravery is courageous behaviour rooted in character. In life, we see a lot of wrongs and all of us have a sense of right but also the fear of addressing what is wrong. When we see something wrong, but stand up despite the fear and speak out, it's bravery. Very few possess this quality and that is what separates the lions from the sheep.

Ideas for Action: As much as possible, have the integrity to stand up and speak out for what is right. No matter who the wrongdoer may be, stand up and speak out. The person or institution you oppose may be very powerful and you may feel like its David v/s Goliath. But still try and stand up as a voice of conscience, as a voice of dissent, against the wrong and feel the power of bravery.

11

Transforming Lives

Kiran Modi

K iran is a Sanskrit word that means 'a ray of light'. This ray has continuously shone all the way through the years, between the dark clouds of adversity to bring the light and sunshine into thousands of lives. Kiran Modi, still with an omnipresent glow on her cheeks that is reminiscent of youthful mothers, has fruitfully transformed a deep personal tragedy and sorrow into unbounded happiness and joy for disadvantaged children through a non-government organization (NGO) that she established in her son's memory – Udayan Care – after her elder son Udayan's untimely death in 1994.

Kiran's son was a student in Washington D.C., USA, pursuing a degree in finance and economics, and he used to stash away the money he got from home. With this salted away money, he supported orphans in Biafra and other African countries. Kiran and her husband Sudhir discovered this while going through Udayan's papers after his tragic death.

Kiran resolved, right away, to continue her son's vision of helping the underprivileged and ignored children. However, though the real-life narration has moved forward, there is a need to step back three decades and peep into the transformation of a happy, contented young student into a dedicated, unswerving and unpaid charitable person determined to make civil society a participant in social change.

Kiran was blessed to be born into a very contented and financially comfortable family in Kolkata. After her high school graduation, her marriage was arranged (as is still quite the practice in India). On moving into her husband's home, she was supported by him as well as her in-laws to continue her studies (quite exceptional, to say the least), which she did, winning gold medals at the graduate and post-graduate levels. Later, she received a PhD in English Literature from the prestigious Indian Institute of Technology, Delhi, on completion of which, her guide, noted poet Padma Shri Sunita Jain, presented her with her own centuries-old gold sovereign, in tacit recognition of Kiran's scholarship and absence of gold medals at the doctoral level.

When faced with a crisis triggered off by a personal tragedy, the inner strength of a person emerges as a coping mechanism. Such an inner strength is shaped by the values assimilated during the growing-up years.

When faced with a crisis triggered off by a personal tragedy, the inner strength of a person emerges as a coping mechanism. Such an inner strength is shaped by the values assimilated during the growing-up years. Kiran's style of dealing with anguish and heartache was instantaneous: to give muscle to the initial efforts of her son Udayan in making a more equitable world.

Thus, the establishment of Udayan Care to 'regenerate the lives of the disadvantaged', especially children as well as women. And how better to regenerate lives than through education? Initially, Kiran established one *Udayan Ghar* – Eternal Sunshine Home – in Sant Nagar in South Delhi for orphan girls. She did this amidst much opposition since such homes were usually set up in isolated areas, rarely if ever, in well-established residential areas, which Sant Nagar was, and continues to be.

Kiran started with a few girls, one of the first of whom (like many others, by now), is happily married. This is an extremely significant affair, since most orphans become unwilling recipients of societal ills, including maltreatment and sometimes, even violent behaviour. Oftentimes, such misdeeds are by close family members and friends. Consequently, an orphan's belief in the family system becomes shaky. Possibly the greatest achievement of Kiran and Udayan Care is re-instating their faith in human relationships, through her warm, loving and stimulating leadership of mental health specialists, social workers and full and part-time volunteers who take up the responsibility of 'regenerating the rhythms of life' of such children. Indeed, it has developed a whole new understanding in India about group foster care and positive mental health programmes. Today, Udayan Care's forethought on the issue, along with advocacy efforts by other NGOs, has led to the insertion of a whole section on positive mental health in Juvenile Justice Act and how it is mandatory for all childcare institutions.

Kiran started slow, one *ghar* or home at a time, and slowly expanded so that today, after almost two decades, there are thirteen homes, and three aftercare facilities; some for boys and the rest for girls (under the Indian law, it is necessary to have separate homes for boys and girls). These homes started in Delhi and its surrounding areas of Gurgaon, Noida and Greater Noida and then spread their wings to Kurukshetra and Jaipur, both cities being a few hours' drive away from the national capital.

Are these *ghars* distinct and different from the usual homes being run elsewhere? Definitely. Kiran has started a new concept: differentiating between a biological mother and a mentor mother (one who is *like* a mother), and later introducing even mentor fathers. She sought out well-established ladies of substance, those who had 'parented' successfully with entrenched extended families, and confronted them with the challenge of parenting all over again. Since these homes were designed like customary middle-class homes, she decided to limit each home to a maximum of 12-13 children. This too received criticism for not being a cost-efficient model. Kiran went ahead nonetheless.

Since education had shaped her own personality and given her self-respect and self-esteem, she was categorical that the children be sent to the best possible schools – usually referred to as public schools. It was an uphill task, but passionate yet level-headed arguments with the school authorities won the day. And it continues even today.

Udayan Care children study at the best-known schools. They are tutored by dedicated volunteers, teachers and of course, the mentor mothers. Although, often handicapped by the absence of initial educational milestones, the children respond in an adequate manner and in due course bring credit to themselves and their schools. They carry on with college or vocational education, and stand well on their own feet. This is best reflected in the fact that all the *ghar* children, at a workshop, voluntarily decided to adopt the universal surname Udayan. So, they are now Ritu Udayan, Salma Udayan, and Sachin Udayan.

Twelve Udayan *ghar* girls have been on travel fellowships to Singapore and the USA. On being interviewed by a local San Francisco TV channel on how she found the USA, Ruhi had answered with a grin, "Cool, man!" Marjina and Shivani had charmed listeners on the Australian radio network. Such is the self-confidence, poise and buoyancy of spirit of the Udayan children.

Reflecting on such a bright and breezy spirit, Udayan Care's former mentor mother, late Teji Singh Anand, a distinguished and retired school principal had mused, "I thought I knew it all, but with these children, I learn something new about human nature, every day!" Another mentor mother Usha Singh enthuses, "I don't know about regenerating the lives of our children, but the lives of my family and I have surely been regenerated." Madhu Gupta, who facilitated the setting up of the first Udayan Boys' Home, reminisces, "After doing a bit of community service on my own, and in different organizations, I felt that this is the programme I would like to be associated with."

Weaving philanthropists into the Udayan Care programmes have been Kiran's another accomplishment. They all confess to having been captivated and mesmerized by her enthusiasm for bringing excellence into the lives of these children. One day, Chanda, the caregiver at the first Sant Nagar home, grandly announced to Kiran that she would commit suicide. Her reason: the husband had abandoned her and her own biological children were in an orphanage where education was restricted to state-run schools, which in general perception, were several notches lower than the public schools where Udayan Care children studied. So, if she died, she reasoned that her children could become wards of Udayan Care and would have the advantage of superior schooling and superior grooming for adulthood.

"We must expand to include girls from disadvantaged families," mused Kiran, "though they may have parents, they too need equal opportunities to come up in life." This incident set Kiran thinking – what but a mother's love could imagine such a simplistic solution of suicide to ensure quality education and better future for her children? What happens to the hundreds of girls from poor families who had the ambition of studying? Thus came about the Udayan Shalini Fellowship Programme, which reaches out to such girls.

Shalini in Sanskrit means a fulfilled woman. Twelve years on, the programme has made a difference to over 3,500 girls in eight cities – Delhi, Kurukshetra, Aurangabad, Kolkata, Phagwara, Haridwar, Gurgaon and Dehra Dun. The girls are mentored to excellence, both in academics and life. They are selected after their class X exams, and are supported through their graduation and post-graduation studies. The fellowship – not scholarship, which tends to point towards financial assistance alone – programme has produced a PhD; three medical doctors, over a hundred school teachers and more than twenty engineers. Several of the girls study in the world-renowned Indian Institutes of Technology (IITs) and Indian Institutes of Management (IIMs), advanced scientific research institutes and other prominent colleges and universities.

The selection process is unusual and doesn't test the learned knowledge of the girls. Udayan Care's testing system, NAT (for Needs, Ambition and Talent), analyses the examinees through innovatively designed question papers, home visits by trained social workers and intensive interviews with experts. The test has been designed to bring out the inner qualities, secret desires and dreams of the girls. As Payal Taneja, one of the first fellows and now a practicing chartered accountant, says, "Where did I even have the courage to dream?" Her father did not have even ₹50 (less than $1) to buy the application form for the chartered accountancy programme. Today, the fellows have the power to dream, take control of their lives and, most importantly, take over the leadership of their families. They have become medical doctors, management specialists, school teachers, IT specialists and social workers to contribute back to societal upliftment.

Strongly influenced by the role of education in her personal life, Kiran encourages interaction of the fellows with academicians, professors, management experts, motivational speakers and other acknowledged experts in their fields. The mental horizons of the fellows expand in a marvellous manner. "I never imagined I could ever speak and exchange thoughts, on equal terms, with such eminent persons," says Kanika Gupta, an IT engineer who now works with the Infosys. "Udayan Fellowship Programme taught me to respect my own scholarship," gushes Darshana Joshi, a fellow at the programme and a PhD student at the Cambridge University.

Around the time when HIV-positive people initiated new approaches to social work, an area that was not receiving as much attention as it should have was the family arrangement of HIV-negative children of HIV-positive parents. The Damocles' sword of death hung over the HIV-positive people and consequently, their non-positive children would become insecure. Additionally, they were the sufferers of social prejudice. Innovating as always, Kiran initiated a programme for such families.

Over 70 families meet on a regular basis and a trained social worker conducts programmes and helps them form self-help groups. "It is amazing," says Kiran, "to see what peer support can do to similarly afflicted. They care and share with each other and learn coping mechanisms; we become only catalysts and facilitators." The families are given the financial assist to supplement whatever the positive persons are able to earn, while they can. Ill health often leads to absenteeism at work and thus, no earnings. This unusual programme has brought cheer and joy into the lives of these families.

Kiran's ventures have reached out to the neighbourhood, too. It goes back to the times when she established the first home in Sant Naga. The neighbourhood of all middle-class families with a smattering of local offices was initially not very accommodative about an orphanage among them. The reason was rooted in community myths – such children are often thought to be 'child thieves' – *a la* the young hungry child 'robbing' a slice of bread in Charles Dickens's *David Copperfield*. The children were almost ostracized. However, the sounds of laughter and hilarity that are a natural outcome of children living together soon began 'infecting' the houses around and penetrating the hearts of the families. In a few months, the children had become the pride of the area. This infection is contagious, and has successfully spread to all the families where Udayan homes are placed.

Udayan Care has played, and continues to play, a significant role in improving the state of affairs about child rights.

Standing up for the rights of children has been but a natural accompaniment to Kiran's work and commitment. Udayan Care has played, and continues to play, a significant role in improving the state of affairs about child rights. It participates and indeed, leads the way, in positive mental health issues, charter of children rights' concerns and training of caregivers at various levels, volunteers, mentors, professionals and mental health specialists, amongst others.

The continuum in Kiran's life carries on, all in a manner that passes on to the children, the donors and well-wishers, volunteers and staff and all those whose lives touch Udayan Care, completing their lives in the process.

When will it be complete? When He who makes such universal decisions rules that all children will get all the breaks and openings that ensure equity in this wonderful world.

Meanwhile, the ray of light, that is Kiran, will continue to shine... and light up one more such approach.

Biographer

Vikram Dutt wears many hats: disability expert, documentary filmmaker, inclusive and special education consultant, university teacher, journalist and features writer, a sportsperson and a qualified sports coach from the National Institute of Sports, Patiala. He has been active in the passage of several landmark legislations in the social service sector and has initiated work in the field of mental health and well-being of orphans and juveniles, as well as in his primary field of disability. As Secretary of the Board of Management, he helped establish the Indian Spinal Injuries Centre in New Delhi. He is a much-invited motivational speaker. Currently, he is Principal Academics at Delhi Metropolitan Education, a law, journalism and management professional college, affiliated to Guru Gobind Singh Indraprastha University, Delhi.

moJOsh Inspirator Power 11:
The Power of Perseverance
(Includes Passion)

"You may encounter many defeats, but you must not be defeated. In fact, it may be necessary to encounter the defeats, so you can know who you are, what you can rise from, how you can still come out of it."

~ Maya Angelou

Thought Leadership for Reflection: No one in our world is bereft of suffering. Therefore, in some way or the other we all break. When broken, most give up and breakdown. Some, however, refuse to give up and persevere to breakthrough. Our choosing to breakdown or breakthrough is what defines us. Remember passion means suffering. Hence the saying 'No pain, no gain'.

Ideas for Action: Perseverance is persistence, steadfastness, resilience and passion in doing something despite difficulty or delay in achieving success. Never give up and never give in. Remember, you have what it takes to break through. It just requires a little more time, patience, perseverance and integrity not to give up. You are limitless and not limited by a few setbacks and hardships, big or small.

12

Helping Make a Thousand Dreams Come True

Lakshmi Venkatraman Venkatesan

When Pranaya Patil returned to her father's modest home in Saswad village near Pune after her divorce, she could not have dreamt of running a business hiring over forty people in less than ten years. Shailender Singh of Seekri village in Haryana, a farmer's son who had to drop out of college in the very first year to shoulder family responsibilities, started a flour mill with merely ₹25,000 in 1994. He could not have imagined then that he would one day run a ₹40-million enterprise of 2,700 people and that the chief minister would honour him as the Micro-Entrepreneur of the Year in 2007. Likewise, Bhausaheb Janjire, a domestic worker and the son of a bonded labourer, started off with a ₹50,000 loan in 2005-06. Today he runs a ₹250-million business. Pranaya, Shailender and Bhausaheb are but only three of the thousands of Indian stories about the triumph of the human spirit over severe adversity. They also had a common ally during their inspiring journeys – they were all guided by their respective mentors from the Bharatiya Yuva Shakti Trust (BYST) who have over the years stood by them with unfailing encouragement, providing advice and support, as Pranaya, Shailender and Bhausaheb worked relentlessly towards their goal. For Lakshmi Venkatesan, the founder and managing trustee of BYST, their success, like that of hundreds of other entrepreneurs she supports and nurtures, is indeed her own.

Lakshmi herself hails from a privileged background. Indeed, backgrounds rarely get any more privileged than hers. Her father, R. Venkatraman, a most respected figure in Indian politics, was already well-established in the state politics of Tamil Nadu by the time she, the youngest of his three children, was born. He became a minister when she was only four, and that was just the beginning of a stunning career that reached its peak in 1987 when her father became India's eighth President.

But Lakshmi's real endowment was not the power and prestige that came from her father's success, but the values and normalcy of life that the family consciously retained and nurtured while living in the limelight. She had the benefit of awareness without the dependence on the trappings of power. Politics was all around and social issues were a part of their dinner table conversations. She and her sisters grew up on a diet of incessant debates around 'what were the social ills', 'what needs to be done', but only as ordinary citizens and not as people with special privilege.

Like in any middle class Tamil Brahmin home, education was the be-all and end-all of life in the Venkatraman household, and her father's enthusiasm for science, as a tool to serve society, was infectious. It is hardly surprising then that after graduating from Delhi, the young Lakshmi set sail for graduate studies in nuclear physics at the Florida State University in 1974. A Masters in systems engineering from New York University followed and she joined the famed telecommunications research firm Bell Laboratories in New Jersey, where she spent a decade. During her time there, she married a scientist colleague working in cutting edge Material Science and Nanotechnology. All this time, while her father occupied key Cabinet positions, she lived the typical expatriate life, keeping track of the then expensive international calls and carefully planning the rarer-than-desired visits back home.

But Lakshmi had still not found her calling in life. Somewhere deep down her work at Bell Labs, while immensely exciting, was not fulfilling her core values. She felt she had a lot more to give to the world. In 1988, she resigned from Bell Labs. As a consultant in technology transfer, Lakshmi started spending more time in India while actively considering a return – a move generally viewed insane at that time and strongly opposed by many of her Bell Labs colleagues and friends.

Worse, she did not know what exactly she wanted to do. It was clear that it had to be something that had an impact on the poor, but the key idea eluded her. The one thing that eased her torment of that uncertainty was a lesson her father had taught her – to follow her heart and passions rather than chalk out grand plans; to light a small flame if possible, but not to plan a forest fire. Nevertheless, Lakshmi was eager for a cue to her future. That cue was to come finally, at one of the most unlikely of places.

Mentors form the backbone of the BYST model and BYST dedicates significant resources in preparing them for their role and in supporting their ongoing development.

The setting could not have been more dramatic. It was April 1990 and Lakshmi was accompanying her parents on her father's state visit to the UK. He was already in his eighties so one or two of the daughters or the older grandchildren usually went with the couple just to make sure they were comfortable. They had arrived at the Buckingham Palace and after the formal reception by the Queen, joined the royal family for an intimate lunch. Lakshmi was seated next to Prince Charles. The conversation, in due course, veered to the Prince's Youth Business Trust (PYBT), his brainchild to help young people going through the angst of the Thatcher years –helping them to help themselves rather than as a charity or pure philanthropy. The private sector could help the youth in need, not by hiring them, but by mentoring them in setting up their own businesses. Here was an innovative developmental model that married the humanism of a welfare state with the efficiency of capitalism. And it had already started to show results. The Prince specifically talked about a Muhammad Dattu, an Indian-origin man from East Africa who had become a millionaire in merely six or seven years.

To Lakshmi, the idea came as a raindrop on parched soil. The parallels drawn between the Thatcher-era Britain and a developing India struggling with poverty and unemployment were too obvious to miss. And she knew first-hand what difference mentorship could make. Having the odd distinction of being one among a handful of female engineers in the male bastion of Bell Labs, she was often called upon to mentor women students from Columbia or New York University so that they could become engineers. Moreover, her father had always been a patron of the small and medium enterprises in Tamil Nadu. Suddenly all the pieces seem to fall in place. She could make a difference in India the same way the Prince is attempting in the UK – only on a more diverse scale. The potential for the model was truly unlimited in India as was the crying need for it. Of course, India-sizing any solution was a massive challenge. But Lakshmi was unfazed by that. She knew she should think only of lighting a flame, she could not plan the forest fire.

The excitement was hardly one-sided. Over the next few days, as Lakshmi and the Prince discussed the idea several times, she found him inspirational. And Lakshmi received a lot of material about how the PYBT was run. An idea, and a connection, was born. But it was just that – an idea. Clearly, it seemed to be the right thing to be tried out in India and the Prince was obviously interested in a replication of the concept in a far more challenging context, but questions remained. Would the model work in India? What would it take to find suitable mentors and sustain their interest? How to identify potential entrepreneurs with great ideas and the commitment to make it happen? This was still pre-liberalization India and entrepreneurship was hardly a buzzword. At the small-and-medium enterprise (SME) level, business was for people who failed to secure jobs. A few stunted attempts by financial institutions notwithstanding, venture capital was virtually unheard of in the country. Even abroad, Silicon Valley was years away. Lakshmi was about to take on the hardest challenge in enterprise-building – helping the uninitiated, resource-less, connection-less individuals convert their half-baked ideas into reality. She herself had never worked actively in the SME sector and was returning to the country after a gap of more than a decade. Giving shape to the idea – one of its kind in the Indian setting – would be a massive challenge. But if it worked, it could dramatically change lives of people in need and generate employment for thousands. Lakshmi was willing to give it more than just a shot; she would go for it with all she had.

Lakshmi went to work immediately on her return, setting up BYST. Given the role of the private sector in the model, she bounced the idea off her friends and contacts in the Indian business world and within weeks managed to set up a meeting of about a dozen industry leaders with strong developmental interests to formally broach the idea. Surprisingly, there were no naysayers in that meeting; those came later. The late H.P. Nanda, who had pioneered the idea of Corporate Social Responsibility at Escorts in the 1970s was part of it and enthusiastically took up the idea. Lakshmi then approached the late JRD Tata – a doyen of Indian business and himself a champion of mentor – and had him excited enough to accept the role of the chairman of BYST at the age of 86. Other pre-eminent personalities soon joined the board – the late Mantosh Sondhi, a distinguished technocrat, Rahul Bajaj, a renowned industrialist, politician and philanthropist; and Subodh Bhargava, a highly respected businessman. Rahul Bajaj and Tarun Das, the latter a visionary and a leading corporate executive and the then Director General of Confederation of Indian Industry (CII), were instrumental in helping BYST develop a strategic partnership with CII. The first year was a pilot year, starting off with only five mentors and twelve entrepreneurs. However, by the time the Prince of Wales came to India to officially inaugurate BYST in 1992, he was impressed with the results the pilot had produced.

It was clear almost from the beginning that the PYBT model could not be transported unaltered to India; it had to be modified to suit the Indian scene. BYST took little more than the philosophy from the Prince's organization and approached each of these challenges with an open mind, and not with a pre-prepared questionnaire to judge applications that had worked elsewhere or a mentor selection or engagement process that worked well in Britain. These customizations were critical, for over the years BYST has proved to be among the most successful implementers of the idea that has now been tried in close to 40 countries in the world. Reason: BYST provided a local solution to a local problem, unique in its macro and environmental setting.

The massive promise of India's grass-roots entrepreneurs can only be fulfilled if many, many other BYSTs espouse the model.

Relentless hard work ensued – seeking out the underprivileged to bring out their ideas, identifying mentors to nurture these potential entrepreneurs, forging partnerships with banks to give the entrepreneurs a slight advantage in securing that much-needed seed capital. Slowly, under the able guidance of Rahul Bajaj as Chairman and through strategic collaborations with organizations ranging from Tata Steel, Bajaj Auto, IFCI (erstwhile Industrial Finance Corporation of India), to the Assam State Government, BYST has spread from Delhi and Haryana to Tamil Nadu, Maharashtra, Telangana, Assam and Odisha. Over the years, BYST has worked with entrepreneurs from various kinds of backgrounds and circumstances – people with physical disabilities, people from socially underprivileged classes, not to mention poverty and the gender divide.

Most of BYST's entrepreneurs have a modest education. Lakshmi does not think this in itself to be a huge disadvantage though. According to her, "Entrepreneurship and education have no direct correlation. You must have business literacy, not necessarily a college degree."

BYST has actively partnered with leading national banks to provide collateral-free start-up finance to young entrepreneurs. It has recently established a $5 million growth fund to support the 5% of its grass-roots entrepreneurs, who end up with a turnover exceeding ₹1 million, to further scale up their businesses and reach their much higher potentials. Focusing on enterprise finance with a social objective and a conscious slant towards job creation, wealth creation, environmental appropriateness, statutory compliance and good governance, the fund bridges a critical gap in the Indian financial system. It will lead to the mainstreaming of these entrepreneurs, taking them to a stage where they can be the legitimate clients of the commercial banking system or larger venture capital funds.

However, BYST's real support to these entrepreneurs is in the form of mentoring. As Lakshmi puts it, "It's not money alone that will solve an entrepreneur's problems. Guidance and hand-holding are key, too." Mentors, therefore, form the backbone of the BYST model and BYST dedicates significant resources in preparing them for their role and in supporting their ongoing development. This includes formal training and an accreditation scheme that helps formalize and standardize its mentor offerings across the country. However, enabling is just a part of the story; keeping them enthused about their roles is, arguably, the more critical task. Professional recognition goes a long way and BYST treats every achievement of its entrepreneurs as a joint feat of the entrepreneur and his or her mentor.

To further sustain and spread the culture of mentoring, BYST has introduced Mentor Chapters, currently 25 across the country, each comprising between 20 and 50 mentors. As formal, local groups facilitated by BYST, these chapters are not just responsible for all aspects of the mentoring programme

– mentor induction, awareness generation, technical evaluation and counseling – but also for playing a role in entrepreneur selection. In the true spirit of mentoring, these chapters often take up additional initiatives like creating entrepreneur training programmes and supplementing BYST's own efforts.

BYST's role is that of a facilitator, a supporter of enterprise, and its products are the success stories crafted by the entrepreneurs themselves. While its entrepreneurs go forth to win national and global accolades, not to speak of creating significant wealth for themselves and jobs for thousands, BYST stays content in the background, insisting only that the individual mentor who guided the specific enterprise be recognized and honoured. In the success of its entrepreneurs lay its fulfillment of purpose.

The same philosophy extends to the operating side of BYST as well. Having a supporter in the President of India was an undeniable advantage. But not in the way most businesses or NGOs would think of it. BYST never used government connections to own a plot of land or a building in New Delhi or elsewhere. BYST's obsessive focus on its mission of helping entrepreneurs is reflected in its lack of assets of its own. Even 20 years later, it functions out of borrowed space in Delhi and cramped run-down offices in other cities.

In the nearly two decades of its existence, BYST has outreached and counseled 200,000 individuals and helped create 5,000 entrepreneurs. Over 4,000 mentors, most of them from the SME sector, have contributed to this journey. Together its entrepreneurs have created in excess of 250,000 jobs. More than 10% of these entrepreneurs have become millionaires. While on the one hand the microcredit movement has helped millions at the bottom of the pyramid secure a livelihood, on the other hand, venture capitalists and formal financing channels have supported larger businesses, the distinctive contribution of BYST's model lay in serving the 'missing middle' between these two segments.

Its approach has been completely bottom-up in the sense of supporting ideas brought forth by entrepreneurs rather than driving them towards a pre-decided activity.

Despite substantial achievements and garnering considerable recognition – mostly for her entrepreneurs – Lakshmi is far from content today. She knows that BYST has perhaps only shown the way. Scaling it up to make a serious dent on India's poverty and human conditions still remains a distant dream. She does not even think that a single BYST can ever do it. The massive promise of India's grass-roots entrepreneurs can only be fulfilled if many, many other BYSTs espouse the model. Instead of taking pride in it, Lakshmi is frustrated that BYST is virtually the only organization willing to give the mentorship approach, at the grass-roots level, a serious try.

But there is hope. Some of her own entrepreneurs have taken up mentoring in a serious way. Parallel to running her own soft luggage making business, Pranaya Patil today provides vocational training in making soft luggage, beauty parlor activities, *mehendi* and soft-toy making – skills she had herself learnt in her struggle for a livelihood. She has trained over 450 students so far and motivates them to be entrepreneurs like her. Fifteen of her students are now running successful businesses of their own and creating jobs.

Impatient of waiting for other organizations to take up the idea, Lakshmi hopes her own entrepreneurs would one day be her best ambassadors and carry forth India's traditional *guru-shishya parampara*. For no one knows the value of mentorship more than they do. And if this happens, Lakshmi may very well have started a movement rather than an NGO, however big and successful. Even today, she does not plan the forest fire, but simply cannot help dreaming of one.

Biographer

Rajesh Chakrabarti is currently Executive Vice President, Research and Policy, Wadhwani Foundation. He has taught management for over a decade at the University of Alberta, Canada, the University of Georgia Tech, USA, and the Indian School of Business (IBS), besides holding several visiting positions including at the Indian Statistical Institute, Indian Institute of Management Calcutta and the Federal Reserve Bank, Atlanta. As the founding Executive Director of the Bharti Institute of Public Policy at ISB's Mohali campus, he helped design and launch one of India's leading public policy programmes. He has authored/edited six books, with three more in the pipeline, in addition to several articles on finance, economics, and management in international journals. He is a columnist with the *Financial Express* and is frequently quoted in the media. Rajesh is an alumnus of Presidency College, Calcutta and Indian Institute of Management, Ahmedabad, and has his PhD from the University of California, Los Angeles.

moJOsh Inspirator Power 12:
The Power of Honesty

"Honesty is the first chapter of the book wisdom."
~ Thomas Jefferson

Thought Leadership for Reflection: Honesty is about being free of deceit and untruthfulness, about being sincere. The original meaning of honesty had more to do with honour than truthfulness, although the two are naturally linked. The trait of honesty has been prized for centuries, and Shakespeare once wrote, "Honesty is the best policy. If I lose my honour, I lose myself."

Ideas for Action: Honest people have the integrity to understand themselves and know their own strengths and weaknesses. They will not delude themselves about their successes or failures. Honest people present themselves in a way that shows who they really are. Their reputation will be founded on what they are and, whether in public or private, they will be the same. They will meet any commitments or promises that they make and always preserve their honour.

13

Artemis' Calling

Lynn de Souza

The year was 1987. A young 26-year-old Indian advertising professional with an illustrious career ahead of her was travelling by road from Rome to Assisi. It was the month of August, and amid pounding rain, the driver of her coach lost control. The vehicle skid, and in the process hit a hapless dog that had run on to the road from a nearby farmhouse.

The dog was badly injured and hid inside the wheel chamber under the coach. The driver was in a fix. He couldn't move the coach forward, nor was there anybody in the vicinity to rescue the dog for fear of being bitten by the wounded animal. At this juncture, the young passenger of the coach took the split-second decision to rescue the animal herself. Frightened as she was, she managed the deed by crawling under the coach on her back, without thinking twice about her hands and clothes getting covered in the blood of the helpless animal.

It is perhaps no coincidence that she was on her way to visit the birthplace of St. Francis – also known as the patron saint of animals and the environment. The incident and the visit left a deep impact on the young advertising professional's psyche. And throughout her three-decade-long successful career, she would find a constant, recurrent calling to surrender in the service of animals, the voiceless inhabitants of our planet.

Fast forward by several years, St. Francis of Assisi was perhaps not the first thing you would have noticed if you had walked into Lynn de Souza's cabin at Lintas Media Group office in Lower Parel, Mumbai, where she had spent a better part of the last decade. The tiny signature Tau Cross on the wall behind her is the only indication of her devotion to the saint and his teachings.

A national tennis champion, Lynn graduated in economics and then went on to become one of India's first few women management graduates. She spent the first five years of her career at Ogilvy, Benson & Mather, where she did the planning and buying for various powerful brands. In 1988, she joined Grey Worldwide (erstwhile *Trikaya Grey*), which played a crucial role in shaping her professional traits. "Trikaya (Grey Worldwide) was the place to find yourself, while O&M was the place to find your friends," she said.

The more one observes Lynn and her approach to life, the more one can sense the influence of St. Francis in her being. She is among the rare successful professionals who had the privilege of donning several hats of which two, in particular, were diametrically different – one is of a leading figure in the Indian communication business and the other, is of the selfless love and instinctual compassion she has for the welfare of animals. As the years unfolded, the latter would become more prominent in Lynn's scheme of things.

Another distinctive characteristic of Lynn is doing the most unexpected, and often, she turned it to her advantage. One such instance was when at the peak of her career, she took a sabbatical all of a sudden to pursue her other interest, and became a qualified veterinary nurse in Australia. She followed her new calling with the same kind of dedication and passion she showed in her professional life.

Her affection for animals can be traced right back to her childhood. Growing up in a Goan animal-loving household, it was one of her predominant qualities as a young girl. As children, both Lynn and her brother brought stray dogs and other injured animals home. At one point, there were seven dogs in the family of four! Once an animal entered the de Souza household, it never left. Lynn was about nine years old when rescuing animals became a habit of sorts with her, a habit that stayed with her even when she was rushing for client meetings as an agency head many years later. While she was known to be punctual in her ways, over the years, it became no surprise to many if Lynn was an hour late or had to reschedule a meeting because a dog was hurt on the road and she was taking it to a veterinary hospital.

Was Lynn perhaps in her passion for animal care, also finding refuge from the media world and its dark side? Perhaps, but she was not analyzing it in this manner back then. She was only following her heart and doing what she believed in. It brought her peace. In her own way, Lynn was beginning to understand what it meant for her. But the time to act on it was yet to come.

Lynn's hectic, high-powered work life speeded ahead, as she moved on from Grey Worldwide to the Lintas Group. Building rapidly on her reputation of being one of the most accomplished media practitioners in India, as head of initiative media, Lynn was a name to reckon with in the industry. She was a member of the company's board by then, and for a woman to achieve that at that stage, came with its set of challenges.

Lynn's traits of fearlessness and doggedness when she is pursuing a cause are now seen in her fight against other societal ills as well.

However, Lynn knew then that she had to do something more than this, to seek a higher peace that she once felt so many years ago at Assisi. In 1997, a seemingly innocuous religious incident led her to reconsider the values and ethics of society and humanity at large. She withdrew into a self-introspecting period and began to spend many hours at the veterinary hospital in Parel, where she had volunteered to work with horses and at the dog sterilization ward.

Shocking many of her well-wishers, in 1998 Lynn bid adieu to the world of advertising to pursue veterinary nursing at

Ithaca TAFE in Brisbane, Australia. At that point, she was 36 and said to be the highest paid media professional in India.

Away from the industry, she honed a different set of skills altogether, as she laid the foundation to truly making a difference in the field of animal welfare.

Lynn returned to India in 2000 and met Maneka Gandhi, who is also known for her contributions towards the welfare of animals in India. With this, Lynn embarked upon a new journey, where she would set up the Goa Society for Prevention of Cruelty to Animals (SPCA).

Her dream of building a dedicated hospital for animals in Goa exposed Lynn to many newer challenges. Even though Goa was her ancestral home and Lynn had managed to garner support of people who believed in the cause, getting the right staff both in terms of training and commitment was an ordeal. While she was still looking for space, Lynn made it a point to volunteer at the Bombay Society for the Prevention of Cruelty to Animals (SPCA) in Parel to practice her recently acquired skills of a nurse.

Finally, with a base sum of ₹25 lakh, Lynn was able to lead a team that set up an animal care facility, including a veterinary hospital, in Goa. She donated her ancestral property in Torda to build the shelter. For the next four years, the facility consumed nearly 50% of her time to ensure that the basic requisites of the hospital, Socrates Oliver Veterinary Hospital, were in place. The Goa SPCA also worked towards helping other organizations in the state to develop animal care facilities and in spreading awareness about the cause.

In June 2006, the Goa SPCA was accepted as a member society of the World Society for Protection of Animals (WSPA), the largest federation of animal welfare bodies in the world, with consultative status to the United Nations. Since 2010, the shelter has faced several challenges from local residents and the builder's lobby. While Lynn's role in the facility has changed now to more of a mentor, who also funds the operation for the most part, she has made sure that the shelter works without stopping. The facility is both intense work and a getaway for her. Today, she is a person the Indian Animal welfare society recognizes as an active hand to count upon when in need.

Lynn knew the importance of clearly demarcating both her roles much early in her pursuit. Her ambition for the Goa SPCA was not only to take care of destitute animals but also educate people on how to take care of pets. Lynn continues to work actively towards achieving it. She has treated dogs, horses, birds and even a tiger. The impatient lady, who was living life on the fast track, had begun to appreciate the virtues of patience and slowing down. A colleague who has known her for over two decades now remarks, "There is a compassionate, a more human side that has come to Lynn. She has developed the ability to understand issues others are facing even if someone is not confiding in her directly." Lynn writes extensively on animal care issues and related subjects to do all that she can to raise awareness.

Lynn's traits of fearlessness and doggedness when she is pursuing a cause are now seen in her fight against other societal ills as well. She has extended her caring vision to tackle issues of women's rights, children's rights and environment at large. She began to foresee her next calling in 2010 when Interpublic Group of Companies (IPG) requested her to set up the IPG Women's Leadership Network in India. She was tasked with planning ways to recruit and retain the female workforce. Initially, Lynn resisted the task, believing that any form of differentiated treatment as a woman was something she personally never asked for, and didn't want to encourage. However, they went about sending her enough material to make her question that premise, and soon she embarked on another new journey. One that understands that this century will be made or broken by the three Ws – web, weather and women; that the future of our planet is completely dependent on the survival and growth of the female gene and traits in humanity, and that every form of engagement –

corporate, social, military, legal, governmental – will benefit from having women at the helm.

In the meanwhile, Lynn had returned the world of adverting in 2003. In 2012, Lynn did the unexpected, once more. After a four-year term as the chairperson and CEO of Lintas Media Group, she resigned from her position to focus her energies on driving reform through the power of communication. Her next venture was born, India's first communication firm that works for social change, Social Access.

Unlike her passion for animals that had stemmed from her childhood, it was the life that Lynn has observed as a female professional in India and, more importantly, as a citizen of a vastly diverse and changing country, that led her to contemplate issues of larger social significance.

"There comes a time when all that one learns in a memorable career – all the experiences, both good and bad; all the relationships; all the achievements – cry out to be put to a more selfless purpose."
~ Lynn de Souza

"There comes a time when all that one learns in a memorable career – all the experiences, both good and bad; all the relationships; all the achievements – cry out to be put to a more selfless purpose," she said.

After several years at the top echelons of the media industry, in 2013 Lynn spearheaded Social Access, to offer affordable communication strategy and services to NGOs and connect them with corporates houses who are interested in helping their causes. She is currently nurturing a young, ambitious and idealistic team, and in just three years the company has several prestigious projects under its banner.

The firm has executed over 33 projects in this space, working for solar energy, watershed management, education of rural girls, child protection, empowerment of women in advertising, animal welfare, corporate volunteering, marathons for causes, etc., with the support of India's largest media companies to generate funding worth over ₹10 crore. "In a short span, we have produced 22 extremely low-budget, but high-impact films for the social sector," says Lynn.

Over the years, from someone who tried to understand the pain of an animal that could not articulate it, Lynn has developed the ability to understand issues that she may not have been directly subjected to. She has been a recipient of several awards for performance excellence, for her humanitarian efforts and for contribution to the growth of the advertising industry. However, Lynn staunchly maintains that her most cherished award is a grateful smile, or a lick! And that her best is yet to come. "The idea is not about goal-setting anymore. It is doing what needs to be done," she says. Lynn leads by example. She does not just sympathize with a situation but also does something about it.

Biographers

Deepa Krishnan is a business journalist with over a decade of wide-ranging experience in writing on development, environment, culture, society and all things in between – besides, of course, business.

Noor Fathima Warsia is a veteran journalist in the Indian marketing, media and advertising fraternity.

moJOsh Inspirator Power 13:
The Power of Rejuvenation
(Continuous Improvement, Appreciation of Beauty and Excellence)

"We must always change, renew, rejuvenate ourselves; otherwise we harden."

~ Johann Wolfgang von Goethe

Thought Leadership for Reflection: I always tell people that perfection is a myth because the day we are perfect is when we are in the box (called coffin – the box in which our bodies go after we die). I joke with them that if you are perfect, you are dead. Being dead in a box is the perfect state. So, till you are not in that box, stay and remain out of the box and strive for continuous improvement and renewal.

Ideas for Action: If you are alive today, you need to transform, be better and more beautiful in mind, body, heart, spirit and soul today than what you were yesterday. You do not want to be like most people who are just existential; they are walking around and talking but they are already in the box. They are routine; they have settled for the ordinary. Every day gives us an opportunity to appreciate our beauty, rejuvenate and push our potential, in our quest to excel more day by day. Therein lies the law of transformation.

14

Going Social for a Social Cause

Manju Latha Kalanidhi

What makes a social initiative click? Is it a terrific idea or a great plan, huge funding or deep commitment, popular support or elite endorsement, virtual votes or geographical reach? In Manju Latha Kalanidhi's case, it's all of this and then that magical ingredient called love. Love for the cause, for the target population, and for the method or the way things can be done to make a difference.

Come to think of it, it is no surprise that Manju conjured up a wonderful project. People who have worked with her or have been associated with her in a professional or personal relationship would identify some key qualities in Manju that make for a great crusader: sensibility and sensitivity, awareness and attention to what's happening around her, persistence and practical wisdom, and consistency.

The Rice Bucket Challenge is an initiative that was inspired by something else, but went on to become an inspiration of astounding proportions in itself. Months after the concept took off in a spectacular way, Manju remains the same person who had one afternoon randomly posted a tentative idea on social media. She may have been taken aback by the way the challenge spread, but is undaunted and vows to support the cause as long as and as far as it goes.

So how did it all begin? The idea could have come from the famous social media trend, the Ice Bucket Challenge, but the insight was more from the way that challenge was embraced by people across the world. Manju was baffled by the enthusiasm in dumping ice cubes on people's heads by those who seem to have never heard of Amyotrophic Lateral Sclerosis or ALS, leave alone understanding the link between the challenge and the cause.

What followed was initially a simple action – rather like adding an extra letter 'R' before the 'Ice' – of casually posting a challenge on Facebook that seemed like fun but also served a purpose: donate a bucket of rice to a needy person and challenge three other people to do the same. And it set off a chain.

Manju had no expectations whatsoever when she floated the idea. All that she expected was a few polite likes from friends, and, at best, her immediate family taking up the challenge just to please her. But the response to the post was overwhelming, to put it mildly – a whopping 7,000 likes in just one day. And better yet, people earnestly started following it up with donating buckets of rice. The response galvanized Manju into action. A media story the very next day made her realize this was way bigger than she had imagined.

"The first write up about the rice bucket challenge was by a journalist from *The Hindu*. That day almost seemed like God had a checklist to tick off before he gave me this," Manju says. On a day that she calls the 'fateful Saturday', the news of media zeroing in on her work broke amidst the chaos of home repairs, daily chores, power breakdowns, house guests and even an emotional moment of Manju's pet dog Maggie getting badly bitten by a stray. The appearance of the first story was a trigger that set off a deluge and Manju ended up giving more than 200 interviews, including innumerable television appearances, over the next few weeks.

But then media is not a stranger to Manju. A graduate from the Asian College of Journalism, Manju has worked for many mainstream English dailies as a journalist and covered a whole range of subjects that included media itself. She has been living in Hyderabad for 17 years, as much time as she has spent working in the industry.

Born and brought up in Warangal, a sleepy but historically

significant town about 90 miles from Hyderabad, Manju was a part of a regular middle-class family that knew the importance of sensible spending. Her father Narasimha Rao Kalanidhi (who worked with the Indian Railways) and her mom Varalakshmi, a homemaker, ensured that the concept of simple living and high thinking was instilled in Manju and her two older siblings at a very young age.

"There was a time when prominent TV journalist Prannoy Roy was hosting the *The World this Week* on Doordarshan (in the 90s). I used to love the last segment called 'Newsmaker of the Week' with some background music, a bit of information about the person and their work! It was also around the same time that I was determined to sound interesting and even ridiculous in our graduation farewell party at University Arts and Science College, Warangal. So when everyone had to say what they want to do/become in future, I stood up and with tremendous attitude and on a lark, said 'I want to become a sensational newsmaker who is recognized everywhere,'" Manju recalls with a chuckle. Nearly a decade-and-a-half later, that wish came true and how!

"In India, there are millions of people who come under what's the called the 'unorganized sector'. By that I mean they have no health insurance, no job guarantee, no pension. The day they stop working, they may have to go without a meal."
— Manju Latha Kalanidhi

It is a delicious coincidence that Manju actually worked with a website that was entirely about rice. A senior editor with *Oryza*, a global rice news, research and analysis website, Manju relished her job, writing well-researched stories on the subject; a break after a roller-coaster ride through mainstream journalism. "As a part of *Oryza*'s editorial work, I am day in and day out researching about rice, exports, imports, research, shortage, hunger and the like. India itself is a rice-eating, rice-loving country. So the ice-rice connect came in effortlessly," she acknowledges. (*Manju has now moved on to working as City Editor with *The New Indian Express* in Hyderabad.)

The donor Manju chose as the first person in the link is a classic case for food donation. "Sathibabu is a 55-year-old man who sells homemade breakfast to the people in my area. He is a hardworking person and should he ever fall sick, I doubt if anyone would come forward to help him out. In India, there are millions of people who come under what's the called the 'unorganized sector'. By that I mean they have no health insurance, no job guarantee, no pension. The day they stop working, they may have to go without a meal," Manju explains. And it is these people who need a helping hand in their hour of need.

The first four days, after the Rice Bucket Challenge started in August 2014, were the busiest and most overwhelming ones. Her husband Vijeye Devuni, an HR consultant, plunged right into the campaign and began helping out to coordinate and document the responses flooding her Facebook page. Manju concentrated on telling the world about what she wanted to see by way of this challenge. As media pounced on the challenge, sensing a story of amazing content and scale happening right here in Hyderabad, Manju was in a tizzy, turning from one camera to another and explaining the hows and whys of the challenge.

Manju did have to pay a personal price too because of the sheer scale of the response. "Both my husband and I were overworked, overwhelmed, drained out, but still on top of the world. As a single child, my nine-year-old daughter Vanshika never had any dearth of attention and now she had to fend for herself while Vijeye and I were tending to the newborn – the Rice Bucket Challenge!" Manju recalls.

Handling media even as she tackled the logistics of the campaign made Manju realize that she needed a formal office space, assistants, staff and helpers who could deal with the daily tasks. "At some point, I felt I even needed a professional to settle the litigations born out of too many spin-offs of the page, too many fake Facebook accounts masquerading as the Rice Bucket Challenge." Once the tsunami of responses was over, the campaign settled down into a programme, which clearly indicated that it was a winner of the long mile. Vijeye handled the promotions on LinkedIn and Twitter.

So what did she find most interesting about the response? "I was amazed to see absolute strangers across the world – Philippines, Turkey, even Madagascar, who mentioned my name and said they found the Rice Bucket Challenge inspiring. A Russian boy who took up the challenge in Goa moved me to tears. Looking at 2,200 students of Apoorva Degree College in Karimnagar donating 2,200 kg of rice to the needy was an overwhelming movement. It felt like my baby was being honoured there!"

There are many reasons why the Rice Bucket Challenge caught people's imagination. At one go, this concept addresses many aspects of humanity. It reminds people that there is something called hunger in the world, and that there are simple ways to alleviate it, that through a small action that involves negligible financial costs and less time, one can actually contribute towards the most important cause the world grapples with on a daily basis. And because this trouble-free action actually satisfies an urge somewhere deep inside, it sets to rest a social conscience that people have probably been silencing for want of an easy avenue.

"A genuine thought or intention can touch a million people. Social media is a powerful tool and can be a great one to bring out social change. Without spending a penny on advertising or promotions, and just by the sheer strength of a good campaign, one can reach out to millions across the globe. This is what I realized once the Rice Bucket Challenge took off," says Manju.

Where does the challenge stand now? The Facebook page has 64,138 likes, which makes one safely assume that, at least, half of them would have taken up the challenge. Currently very popular in the Philippines and Bangladesh after India, the fame and passion of the Rice Bucket Challenge have spread as far as the US, Australia and Vietnam. Nearly 25 corporate companies from India have taken part in the challenge and each corporate contributes close to 3,000 kg (minimum) making it to 75,000 kg through mass donations alone in one year. There must be at least another 10,000-kg donation that has been done individually. Among individual contributions, the largest has been by Vidya Sagar Panthangi from Hyderabad – 2,500 kg rice in one day. Colleges and corporate employees are among the chunk of donors. Many NGOs and slums of various cities have been the major recipients.

> *"I believe that the Rice Bucket Challenge is akin to a home video shot on a handheld camera that went to join the 100-crore club and got critical acclaim."*
>
> ~ Manju Latha Kalanidhi

The world was quick to recognize Manju Latha Kalanidhi's contribution. Not just media coverage but also many awards came her way. The Just For Woman Achiever Award and the United Nations iCongo Rex-Karamveer Chakra award are the most prominent ones. She was also shortlisted for L'Oreal Paris Femina Social Influencer, #100WomenAchievers of India in 2016 and has been a recipient of the Khushi TV Women's Day award among many others.

Fame, recognition, reach, scale, a sense of fulfillment... Manju has garnered many things from floating one of the most significant ideas of this century, but does that burden her? Does she think people now expect more from her? Does she feel that the mantle of an eternal Samaritan has been foisted upon her?

"I believe that the Rice Bucket Challenge is akin to a home video shot on a handheld camera that went to join the 100-crore club and got critical acclaim. I am not pressurized to make it 'click' further as I feel that something that has lasted for over four months will last for a longer time to come," says Manju.

It is easy to rest on one's laurels. And, in any case, the Rice Bucket Challenge does not need much follow-up, except for the maintenance of the Facebook page. Or does it? Where does Manju see the campaign going?

"Going forward, I want to see it assume a more concrete and physical shape in the form of a food bank or a food connector which effortlessly – through a good network of Rice Bucket Challenge volunteers – connects the donor with the needy. I steadfastly want to say no to direct advertising or spending on any of these things," Manju asserts. "The Rice Bucket Challenge's biggest success lies in the fact that we do not ask people to donate, we inspire them. We do not beseech them, we motivate them," she affirms.

It is expected that people will slowly blend it with their happy occasions as a thanksgiving gesture. "Most rice bucket challenge donations done in the following months have primarily been on birthdays, work and wedding anniversaries and even for break-ups! So, it may take the form of a good gesture on a happy day," Manju feels. As of October 2016, two years since the challenge took off, a conservative estimate shows that over 1.8 lakh kg of rice was generated and reached the poor across the world. The most recent one was of 2,340 kg of rice donated as a part of #SingaporeRiceBucketChallenge on September 23, 2016.

The course of action is clear: take the movement further to more campuses, young people and corporations, take it offline so that those who are not connected on social media can act upon it too, and ensure that the likes, comments and shares translate into actual rice donation.

Even those remotely acquainted with Manju would vouch for her high energy levels, her balanced view of the world and her uncompromising attitude when it comes to doing things she considers important. With the Rice Bucket Challenge, she has put her finger straight on the pulse of a nation that has a hoary tradition of *'anna daanam'* – donation of food – but has almost forgotten about it. In mere three sentences, she has modified what was just a social media fancy into a deed that formed an important link in the sustenance of human population. Share what you have, care for those who have not.

This is a project that is not based on any 'ism'. It has no heavy ideological baggage. Nor does it carry an agenda. It does not involve funding or fundraising. It does not even involve donation in the truest sense of the word. It has no parameters for choosing a recipient except that the person is in need. The touchstone is a desire to do something for someone beyond oneself and the only criterion is a need – an altruistic need on the giver's part and a material need on the recipient's side. It recognizes a primal need in a human being and answers it. Even as it points to gaps in the way our development is shaped. What else can be a more forthright and meaningful charity than this?

Biographer

Usha Turaga Revelli is an independent journalist, passionate photographer and a keen observer of the world around her. She has a way with words when she tells the world what she thinks of it. This closet poet and voice artist loves India and her varied colours, and is always found either travelling or planning a trip. A self-confessed lone ranger, her straight-from-the-heart emotional outpourings on social media have won her many fans that connect with her at a deeper level. The seasoned development journalist is currently with the All India Radio, Hyderabad.

moJOsh Inspirator Power 14:
The Power of Humour

"Good humour is a tonic for mind and body. It is the best antidote for anxiety and depression. It is a business asset. It attracts and keeps friends. It lightens human burdens. It is the direct route to serenity and contentment."
~ Grenville Kleiser

Thought Leadership for Reflection: Many people think humour is just about laughing at a comedy show or a stand-up comic. That is about as humorous as they will ever be. Humour is the quality of being amusing or comical, especially as expressed in literature or speech. Humour is also a mood or state of mind to be light-hearted and learn to laugh at oneself and any situation one may be in. Humour also means having a composed and cheerful view on adversity that allows an individual to see its light side and thereby sustain a good mood no matter what the situation.

Ideas for Action: You love to make people laugh. You have the integrity to focus on the lighter side of life and use your humour to encourage and uplift others. You make the ordinary livelier and put others at ease in times of stress. You learn to be light hearted. Remember, a life without humour is like a bike without shock absorbers. Every little pothole will make your ride seem like hell.

15

Still Standing

Rajinder Johar

Leading a busy life as a senior occupational therapist in King George's Medical College, Lucknow, for good 18 years relieving his patients from agonizing pain and suffering, little did Rajinder Johar know that he, too, one day would be at the receiving end of their fate. "My work involved curing patients with temporary disabilities and providing relief to persons with permanent disabilities, but I had never thought that I would be unceremoniously awarded a 100% disability certificate one day. But then life is governed by the law of uncertainty," says Rajinder.

Rajinder had big dreams for himself and his family: high aspirations, capability, strong will and the dedication to prosper. Destiny dealt him a big jolt on the fateful night of March 30, 1986, when a gunshot injury rendered him a quadriplegic (paralysis of all the four limbs), forcing him to lead his remaining life in bed. However, grit and determination have always remained by his side and he has successfully completed his silver jubilee in that bed.

"A person who has congenital disability never gets to know what he is missing, but a person like me who has already seen 37 springs of life as an able-bodied active being finds it very difficult to accept that he will be spending the rest of his life as a quadriplegic," recalls Rajinder of his initial struggle. Knowing how the rain feels on your face, the earth beneath your feet, the breeze blowing against your body and not being able to feel it anymore; being aware of the beauty of nature – the flowers and the trees, the stars, the sun and the moon, the mountains and the rivers and the sea – but not being able to enjoy them now hasn't deterred a tough Rajinder from enjoying the small pleasures of life.

People who came to see him soon after the tragedy told him that he wouldn't survive for long. He was depressed and disappointed with the turn his life had taken, and he, too, didn't want to live anymore. While waiting for that eventuality, he got extremely bored of the way he had started leading his life – aimless. "But instead of crying and mulling over my fate, I thought that if God hasn't taken my life yet, He must be having some purpose behind it. My mission on earth is yet not finished," he recalls. He started thinking about how to utilize his intact faculties for the betterment of other persons with disabilities. In Rajinder's words, "In those days, I had a strange feeling, I always felt as if I were wading through troubled waters, but after I took a decision as to what I should do, I felt as if I had found the shore."

"Instead of crying and mulling over my fate, I thought that if God hasn't taken my life yet, He must be having some purpose behind it."
~ Rajinder Johar

"I had no movement left in my fingers so I started looking for a writing device but could not find anything suitable. Eventually, my elder brother, Surinder, made an indigenous writing device for me using plaster of Paris and a compass from my children's geometry box. It worked. The device is tied to my wrist with an ordinary bandage and I can write with the help of shoulder movement I wrote many letters but only one, sent to Mother Teresa seeking her blessings for starting a voluntary organization, and received a reply. Thus, I launched Family of Disabled (FOD)," shares Rajinder.

He further adds, "I was already pronounced 100% disabled, meaning I was good for nothing and was going to live the rest of my life as a vegetable. But I wanted to assess my disability on my own parameters as I agree with the view of Walter Bagehot who said that the greatest pleasure in life is doing what people say you cannot do. Moreover, I had nothing left to lose." Fate could not snatch his great sense of humour either. Rajinder compares his life to a movie. He says, "The film-maker (read: God) has divided my life in two parts: pre- and post-accident. The protagonist is the same but the role has changed." He goes on to say, "Earlier I could only sympathize with persons with disabilities but after becoming disabled myself, I have started empathizing with them. I wanted to connect with other people with disabilities in the times when technology wasn't, so advanced as I realized there were hardly any sources. So I introduced *The Voice.*" It was the country's first magazine on disabilities to fill the void of such literature in magazine format and also to meet the demand of persons with disabilities, rehabilitation professionals, educationists and others interested in the subject. He jokingly says, "*Bandar lakh boodha kyun na ho jaye lekin gulati khana nahin chhorta.*" (A monkey may age by several years, but he doesn't leave somersaulting.) Rajinder utilized all the knowledge and experience that he had gained over the years as an occupational therapist. He was responsible for editing as well as publishing of the magazine. His nephew sponsored the first edition.

"I also started organizing get-togethers for interaction among persons with disabilities. This way, I was able to establish contact with a large number of persons with disabilities from different walks of life – rich and poor, educated and illiterate, confident and weak. Together we felt like a prodigious family, which explains the nomenclature of the organization," he remembers fondly.

One of the most active members, Rohini Krishnan, belonged to an affluent family. Her father once visited Rajinder and found him quite depressed and tensed about the publishing of the forthcoming issue of the magazine due to lack of funds. Rajinder's passion ignited compassion in him and the very next day, Mr. Krishnan's driver arrived with the cheque and a letter of commitment from him to support the publishing of *The Voice*. Mr. Krishnan has been supporting the printing cost of the magazine since then.

Rajinder understood the needs of disabled people and has thereby been able to introduce a variety of programmes for their welfare. One such innovative idea came to his mind, when Jitender Kumar, a victim of terrorism in Punjab, approached him in 1993, disillusioned with his life. His own brothers ill-treated him and his parents could not support him much. He had come with high hopes to Rajinder and said, "I want to be economically independent, what can you offer me?"

"I have never drawn a penny from the organization saying that I don't need it but Jitender made me realize how important financial independence was for most of the persons with disabilities, who are living below the poverty line and are unlettered and unskilled," shares a concerned Rajinder. "I shared my trepidation with Surinder, my elder brother, who was working in a public-sector unit. I requested him to collect funds among his colleagues, which could be invested in a small public call office (PCO) and snack booth. Around ₹2,500 was raised to buy products for the booth," informs Rajinder.

Jitender visited Rajinder regularly for guidance in running the trade and Rajinder mentored him. Jitender succeeded and flourished. He had led a miserable life in the refugee camp. He had always faced humiliation at the hands of his own family members for not being financially independent. But now, he is capable of looking after the basic needs of food, clothing and shelter of his family and is also able to afford good education for his children. Today he has many fixed deposits in the name of his two children and has secured their future. Not only has he bought a house in Delhi but has also purchased a residential plot in Punjab from his savings.

"But even after this success, I felt helpless as I could not replicate this process due to lack of funds. Now my struggle began to find a way to generate funds. I connected with an artist having quadriplegia, got some designs made, translated them into greeting cards and started marketing them over the telephone," recalls Rajinder. He took the help of volunteers where legwork was required. Every year, he tried finding new artists, to help them gain recognition and remuneration for their skills, and kept depositing the amount generated from greeting cards.

With the little money saved, Rajinder launched Apna Rozgaar Scheme (ARS), a self-employment initiative for those persons with disabilities who were poor, unskilled and illiterate as he found them to be the most marginalized. "Even the 3% reservation in government and public sector jobs could not do them much good as those jobs required educated people," he snaps. Soon, he realized that there were many persons with disabilities who needed his help and he would not be able to generate enough funds through the already diminishing market of greeting cards. He approached funding organizations and individuals to support the programme. He was amazed to see people jump with excitement at the idea of ARS. It was so simple and yet no one had ever thought about it before. They gave him his wholehearted support. Funding organizations like Trickle-Up, Charities Aid Foundation, RC Malhotra Foundation Trust and Give2Asia have funded the programme, which has reached hundreds of persons in dire need. The return on investment makes it the most popular social initiative. There are many individuals who haven't met Rajinder but are deeply moved by his passion and contribute freely to the cause that he has dedicated his life to. FOD now gives a soft interest-free loan of ₹4,500 in kind to an ARS entrepreneur and give full freedom to the incumbent to choose the trade.

Rajinder's strenuous efforts led to the identification of many artists with abundant talent who hitherto had been waiting for an opportunity but were unable to find them on their own. Majority of them being speech and hearing impaired have communication barriers, many are physically disabled and not in a state to run around to promote themselves. "For the artists, their skills are the only source of livelihood – a matter which has always been of prime importance to me. I tried contacting many reputed galleries for exhibition of the artworks but with no success. My efforts yielded results only when I came across Arpana Caur, herself an artist of international repute," says a relieved Rajinder. His message left on voicemail received a positive reply. She agreed to host the exhibition for that year and for the years to follow. Impressed by his persona, a shy individual like her, too, could not hold herself back from paying him a visit. Since 2001, FOD has been organizing an annual exhibition at the Academy of Fine Arts & Literature with the support of Arpana Caur, who not only donates her gallery space but is also magnanimous enough to curate the exhibition and encourage her friends to buy the artworks. "The canvas of Beyond Limits has expanded manifold since its inception. We work hard to identify and reach out to the deserving artists living in remote places of India and offer them this unique platform to earn recognition and appreciation apart from monetary gains," he explains.

The annual exhibition does not satisfy Rajinder; he is constantly looking for other avenues of promotion for these artists and has been successful in organizing exhibitions of their authentic artworks in other galleries as well. His interaction with many disabled people brought him in touch with skilled artisans who were living in poor economic conditions. He always tries to market their products through stalls in corporate fairs. "I connect them with buyers and fetch them orders that support them," he says.

Rajinder's deteriorating health doesn't allow him to move anywhere from his immediate surroundings. His disability hasn't deterred him from following the path that he has chosen for himself. On the contrary, he says, "This life is a blank cheque; it is on us what we would fill it up with." He cashes in every minute that is left with him. "Though confined to my bed, I understand the importance of rejuvenation and recreation for persons with disabilities and organize the same especially for school-going disabled children, who feel left out and depressed when their non-disabled counterparts talk about the historical or educational places that they have seen," shares Rajinder about the annual excursion that he organizes.

He has voluntarily taken upon himself the responsibility of bettering the life of disabled brethren. He doesn't take any grant from the government and instead, raises funds from individuals and organizations to meet the expenditure incurred to benefit persons with disabilities. "I always wanted to mobilize and involve more and more people in my mission without making them feel the pinch on their pockets. So, I came up with an indigenous scheme of collecting old newspapers, electronic gadgets, clothes, etc., as donation and then selling them to their respective dealers to generate funds," says Rajinder. He continuously strives to add more donors to the list by making calls from the phone he keeps by his side to connect to the world. FOD is able to generate at least ₹50,000 every month due to his strenuous efforts. "This money is utilized to educate and self-employ persons with disabilities who are living in poor socio-economic conditions and cannot afford such important facilities on their own," he further adds.

His disability hasn't deterred him from following the path that he has chosen for himself.

"We also give a variety of aids and appliances to persons with disabilities making their daily life comfortable and less dependent. Majority of gadget recipients are either students, petty traders or hitherto neglected cases but beggars are not provided any aid," says Rajinder. Very recently, Rajinder and his team identified a group of eight persons with disabilities, who were operating PCO booths from tricycles, owned by a mafia, near Old Delhi railway station. After labouring for 16 hours a day, all they were left with were ₹100. Rajinder brought them benefit under the two FOD schemes – the ARS and aids and appliances disbursal. They were provided with tricycles as well as a soft loan to buy the products for the trade. The same people are now leading an independent and fearless life. They are able to earn thrice the amount, plus they own the infrastructure. They are able not only to sustain themselves but also financially support their dependents back home. The newly found freedom has provided them peace, health and a vision for a better future.

Rajinder's life revolves around the organization that he has founded. Around 95% of his daily activities are related to the work and why should they not be. He says he has survived for 26 long years because he enjoys his present work far more than what he was doing previously as an occupational therapist. Here he quotes James Allen, "A man sooner or later discovers that he is the master-gardener of his soul, the director of his life." He says, "I discovered this exact thing after my accident. My work has a therapeutic effect on my otherwise failing physical condition." He has a very limited family life. But, at the same time, he gives his family full marks in taking care of all his needs. Although, he never mentions that he has kept his needs to the bare minimum.

Being an occupational therapist, he was well aware how important exercises were for him but he never let his family know. He never wanted to add more pressure on his already over-burdened wife, a banker. She was the sole breadwinner as well as the homemaker. The financial responsibility of fulfilling the basic needs of the family, children's education, running the household, looking after her husband's medical bills were all on her shoulders while Rajinder looked after the kids and their education.

His other love is food. He is always watching cookery shows on television and then wants them to be tried out in his kitchen. He also loves to dote on his granddaughter – the only person who reserves the right of disturbing him even when he is on an extremely busy schedule and in whom he sees a future successor to the work he so lovingly started.

"I have been running the organization from my own house. I started with my bed and then expanded the office to my room and gradually to the first floor of my 150-square-yard residence. All these years of our existence we have been trying to save money for our own multi-purpose rehabilitation centre for persons with disabilities. Now, after almost two decades since the inception of the organization, we have invested all our funds in a plot in Najafgarh area of semi-urban outer Delhi. Through this centre, we will continue our signature style of offering those facilities and training, which have been practically hitherto non-existent but invaluable for persons with disabilities to lead an independent and dignified life," he says.

Rajinder Johar is not just a firm believer but also a shining example of leading from the front. And as John Quincy Adams said, "If your actions inspire others to dream more, learn more, do more and become more, you are a leader." We salute him for turning tables on his disability and inspiring millions of other disabled and non-disabled persons to outreach their limitations and go for the bigger purpose in life.

Biographer

Preeti Johar is the daughter of Rajinder Johar and the CEO at Family of Disabled. She is the driving force behind the organization.

moJOsh Inspirator Power 15:
The Power of Zest

"It is in the compelling zest of high adventure and of victory, and in creative action, that man finds his supreme joys."

~ Antoine de Saint-Exupery

Thought Leadership for Reflection: Zest means great enthusiasm and energy. Zest is about having a quality of excitement and spiciness in life. Zest is a dynamic power that is directly related to physiological and psychological wellness. This power has the strongest ties to overall life satisfaction and a life of engagement. Zest is how you approach all experiences with excitement and energy. You never do anything halfway or half-heartedly. For you, life is an adventure.

Ideas for Action: Nothing should keep us down. We should have the integrity to maintain high energy, excitement and enthusiasm to take action optimistically. Nothing path-breaking can ever be achieved without positivity, optimism, enthusiasm and zest.

16

One Tea Bag

Subha Tampi

From a luxurious penthouse overlooking the azure blue Atlantic Ocean to the dusty dirty streets of Delhi – that's the story and struggle of a courageous woman, Subha Tampi, who fought all odds, kept her sanity, values and hopes and rose inch by inch to earn a name for herself while returning back to society.

The civil war in the West African country of Liberia broke out quite suddenly and came as a shock to many of the locals, let alone the expatriate community living there. Caught in the turmoil, there were some horrifying days when even food and water were a luxury. In fact, there was one point, as the situation there worsened, when Subha and her family had to share a single tea bag between themselves for a number of days. The basic necessities had started to deplete while the gunshots grew louder; plundering, looting, death and disease drew closer with every breath, forcing them into a self-inflicted house arrest.

Armed with just the clothes on her back, her passport and her two small children, Subha finally was able to flee Liberia and come to India leaving behind all her belongings, years of memories and above all that, her husband. Being the general manager of a reputed bank there, he was not allowed to leave the country as the incumbent President of the country was just one amongst a number of very influential people who were the bank's clients. Alone and helpless, she came to Delhi knowing that Kerala, from where she originally hailed, would hold less opportunity for work. Additionally, many of her "friends" who once craved her attention turned the other way when they realized that from the lap of luxury she had been relegated to the status of a poor refugee.

For a couple of years after she arrived in India, Subha was left with little option but to take the aid of a few old acquaintances who still cared and some new ones who understood her plight. "I am living on human kindness and a smattering of hope," – this is what she would say albeit with a hint of irony infused with whatever humour she could muster up during those times. From *barsatis*, to the guestrooms of generous souls, to the ladies waiting rooms of the Delhi railway station on a couple of occasions, she would shift continuously from one accommodation to another, grateful only for the roof over her head. The little bit of savings that she had were spent on putting her children into boarding school and keeping them as far away from the hand that fate had dealt her and her family.

During her many years in Africa, Subha had spent a lot of time immersed in voluntary work for many causes – from orphan children, to handicapped persons and even with lepers. During that time, it was her doing the charity. Little did she know that the day would come when she would be at the receiving end.

A woman of many hats, Subha was considered many things – a professor of literature, a writer, a poet, even an artist, but, of business and industry, she knew not more than what she read in the newspaper. And yet in her time of need, it was this least likely option that revealed itself to be the silver lining she was looking for.

She joined the Confederation of Indian Industry (CII), an established business association, at the bottom of the ladder as an executive assistant, and from there on, it was an uphill climb. The first few years were spent in learning the ropes, understanding the Indian economy, the political establishment, the diplomatic community and everything else required to build a network that would help take the association forward. But life was not easy for this lone young woman battling life in a sometimes cruel society where one was judged by where they stayed and what car they drove.

In the beginning, it meant hours of waiting in the corridors of bureaucrats, ministers and corporate leaders, begging for appointments and two minutes of their valuable time. Through the sweltering summers and the freezing Delhi winters, she would keep at it, and eventually, she learnt the names and knew the backgrounds of all their secretaries, their peons and some of their drivers as well, sharing an occasional cup of tea with them, only to be told every once in a while that the 'minister' was too busy to meet her or the 'CEO' had to rush out for an important appointment. It was during those days that she really came to understand the importance of a kind word or a good deed however small, be it an understanding smile from a secretary or a hot cup of tea offered by the peon on a wintery day, as she waited fighting off the biting cold wearing the only coat she owned at that time. Determination and desperation pushed her on every day and eventually the doors began to open for her.

> "Being a woman is not a weakness at all if we women decide so. We need to understand our strengths and have the courage to build on them."
> ~ Subha Tampi

In the meantime, her husband managed to escape from Liberia and eventually made his way to his family. He had been through a gruelling period, had been tortured, and it took a long time for many of those wounds, both physical and mental, to heal. So Subha became the sole breadwinner for the family, and the 'soul' support for him.

Subha's strong work ethics and ability to achieve results did not go unnoticed and she steadily rose up the ladder making a name for herself – a rare feat for a woman fighting the odds in a sector dominated by men. "Being a woman is not a weakness at all if we women decide so. We need to understand our strengths and have the courage to build on them. The beginning was not just difficult it was tough, to say the least. But eventually, they learnt to look beyond me as just a woman and respect me for my intellectual abilities," says Subha.

As her career graph peaked, Subha still managed to find time to devote to the social sector. Along with various NGOs, she travelled to some of the most deprived areas in India – villages disconnected from the rest of the country – looking for ways to make a difference. One of the key causes that are very close to her heart is that of the girl child. Despite her educational background and a supporting family, she still found it difficult to make her mark in the society. Moreover, every day she would hear or see instances of young girls fighting tougher battles and very often losing them. Tales of female infanticide and cruelty seemed unending.

She has worked hard to achieve everything she has, but changing someone's life for the better meant more to her.

While this really disturbed her, it was an incident during a visit to a small village in Haryana that made Subha start working on this cause. As she stood there taking pictures with some of the villagers, she noticed a small girl being pushed aside by one of the elders. "Go away. You will spoil the picture!" an old man shouted at her. Subha ran to the child and pulled her back. As her face turned towards Subha, she saw the reason for this antagonism. The girl's face was burnt with little left untouched. Her hands and feet were scarred as well. Her name was Bubbly, and yet there was nothing bubbly about the child whose tearful eyes revealed only sorrow. The story eventually came out that soon after she was born, Bubbly 'accidently' fell into a cauldron of boiling water. But she survived and then on for her, every day was a new fight for survival. Moved by her story, Subha decided to do something about it. She wrote a poem on the girl and sent it to some friends and acquaintances just to create a little awareness. They were so moved by the poem that they offered to fund the entire cost of the reconstructive surgery. This changed Bubbly's life forever, giving her a chance to make her name more than just a random word.

One day, Subha saw a young five-year-old girl, Anjali, near her house behind a temple. Despite her rags and dirty disposition, this girl had more wits about her and a smile that could charm a flower. Subha took to her at once and decided that she would take care of the child's education and her basic needs. Overnight, the girl's life changed. Living on the streets with an abusive father, Anjali now has a chance to weave her own story.

The guard of the same temple, asleep near the footsteps, was run over by a drunk truck driver. He died instantly leaving behind a young widow with a six-month-old infant and a three-year-old. Subha, upon hearing this, sprung to action and set up a fund using various social networking tools like Facebook to highlight the case and draw attention to the grief-stricken family. Within days, she managed to collect enough to cover the expenses of the family and the education of the children, and also get the young mother a job.

Recently, Subha found an erstwhile prominent lawyer, who had worked in the UK, abandoned and helpless at a shelter for the homeless. The man, whom she fondly calls Raj Uncle, lost everything after a fire tore through his home and reduced everything he owned to ashes. Along with Brigadier Sanjay, an old friend of Subha, she took the old man to her house. She took care of him and finally found him a job in the school of Martin Howrad, an English man living in Haryana. Raj uncle now lives there in peace, teaching English to the village children and helping in the school administration.

For Subha, experiences like these are her real victories, not the banquets with presidents and kings or the awards and accolades. She has worked hard to achieve everything she has, but changing someone's life for the better meant more to her. "The hot chai with the peon meant more to me than any of these lavish dinners," insists Subha.

Subha has been working with animal welfare organizations and other social organizations where she has taken up the cause of underprivileged sections of the society in different ways. She even started counselling foreign prisoners in Delhi's Tihar Jail. A key reason for volunteering to do this was a sense of empathy. Living in a foreign land where your fate ceases to remain in your hands is something she understands very well.

From riches, she came to rags, and with that she was able to identify her strengths and used them not only for herself but for her family as well as society. She struggled to get back on her feet keeping her reputation and her humility intact through it all.

You may wonder how I know all this. Well, I would, for I am her daughter.

Biographer

Parvati Tampi is a communication specialist and journalist by profession, but an actor, dancer and traveller by passion. Brought up in Africa and having lived in different countries around the world, her life and work are defined by her multicultural background. An Erasmus Mundus scholar, she has mainly worked in the non-profit sector and written on a variety of social issues. Her research in developmental communications led to the publication of a book on the subject of communications towards sustainable development in India. She lives in New Delhi.

moJOsh Inspirator Power 16:
The Power of Love
(Includes Social or Emotional Intelligence)

"You need power only to do something harmful, otherwise love is enough to get everything done."
~ Charles Spencer "Charlie" Chaplin

Thought Leadership for Reflection: Love means a great interest and pleasure in something and a genuine interest in people, animals and nature we encounter in our day-to-day lives. Love is sincerely caring for everyone else's wellbeing. You build relationships of trust sincerely in your personal and personal life. You love yourself, know yourself, manage yourself and your relationships. That is love.

Ideas for Action: You are a people person. You feel close to others, care deeply and express warmth and compassion for people you meet in your journey of life. You have the integrity to put other's needs before your own and take pleasure in being able to foster good relationships. You have people in your life who care deeply about you, but also be sure to leave enough love to care for yourself.

17

Walk Of Life

Sumithra Prasad

I look back and reminisce. The dots are clearer now and Sumithra's life has indeed traced a line that connected all these dots that eventually led to her calling. And her destiny.

It was a mildly cold February morning when we first went out. She had agreed to go with me on a drive. We were cruising on the newly laid highway. As she was intriguing me with her knowledge on varied subjects, I spotted a mangled corpse of a dog on the road. I veered the car around to move on. But she asked me to stop, pick up the remains and move it to the side so that more vehicles don't run over it. She said that even a corpse can't be repeatedly run over. It was a queasy experience but something that made me happy after I pulled it over.

As I returned to the car, she picked my hand up to thank me for the gesture. As she held my hand, I realized it was a very special woman sitting next to me.

As admirable as her noble intentions was her ability to push people to step beyond their comfort zone to do good deeds. Instantly, I knew that she was a woman who had depth in character, possessed inner strength in abundance and could motivate people to go in the direction she wants them to go.

After a few years, we were sitting on the beach with waves repeatedly lashing the shores. The waves followed each other like a bevy of heavy thoughts. And then, she spelt out her moment of calling.

She wanted to quit her current profession of making

corporate films and work with NGOs. Even as I was considering what she said, she slipped past and walked up to a couple of young boys who I guessed were into something juvenile. I could see terrified looks on their faces as she spoke to them. This was followed by nods of approval. A few days later, I answered the doorbell to see the same boys ganged up and asking for her. As I was preparing myself for a stint of heroism, she came by and announced that they have organized a welfare camp. The seemingly unruly boys were fronting the effort to help a marginalized tribal community. Her ability to take up any issue and also channelize the unspent energy of people around her to achieve positive results is amazing.

She steadfastly evangelized the habitat to accept a set of adults with special needs to run a business model from home. Each individual was empowered and assigned a role. They were made to work as a team.

Grains of sand kept trickling down the hourglass. She travelled the length and breadth of this vast country making documentaries for NGOs to create awareness and raise funds. A few weeks back during a spring cleaning session, I started putting the CDs and DVDs of her films. The collection exceeded 250. It speaks volumes of the limitless energy with which she has been continuously making films.

Her arm was in a sling when she tirelessly sought assistance for the tsunami victims. She mobilized volunteers and inspired hundreds of people to contribute to the cause. I couldn't help but have mixed feelings when she came up and asked me to let her travel to the south for helping out the relief team. The doctor had advised her complete rest to recuperate, but she travelled and for reasons beyond me, returned with a smile and without the sling. She draws strength from what she does.

One of the boys, Girijesh Pandey, who accompanied her said, "She was a like the lighthouse... standing tall in all adversity and showing us the way. Doing good never felt so good. I may pursue a profession for my material needs but I'll never be absent from being there for a cause."

The other day she left her mobile phone in my custody. Preeti, a woman from Punjab called. She wanted to discuss the community-based rehabilitation programme for people with disability and also about the workshops in the areas of women empowerment. She wanted to invite Sumithra for the follow-up programmes after the orientation. She said, "Sumithraji's unrelenting attitude, grasp of ground realities and spontaneity to always come up with the right response to a challenging situation has given me a fresh lease of energy. She has given me the belief that the path is right ahead. And being a woman is not an obstacle anymore to make a difference in the society."

I made a note.

The next call was from a teenage girl with an addiction problem. I realized that Sumithra was on a hotline for counseling and support. Another woman running a home for the aged from the marginalized section of the society called to confirm the time for her home visit. In between, there was a call from Kashmir, the caller seeking dates to set up the motivational and capacity building workshops. I had to tell them that she was attending an advocacy rally to sensitize the government on access and rights issues. Subsequently, she had to collect sleeping mats from donors and deliver them to a suburban school set up for destitute children. After this, she had to get back in time to teach our autistic son his political science lesson.

And I did promise that she would call them the minute she returned.

It was an important day for me as I realized how essential she was for so many people. In Kashmir alone, apart from doing a series of workshops, Sumithra coordinated a monumental task of rebuilding a village in the valley that had been ravaged by floods. In what I call a colossal effort, she single-handedly mobilized a ton of relief material, coordinated with the Indian Air Force and airlifted the stranded villagers to other villages in Kashmir.

And yet she has been a meticulous mother, caring wife and committed family member. While on the subject of our son, I need to mention the incalculable effort she has put in to give him the very best. Apart from being autistic, he battles multiple physiological and behavioural challenges. Her steadfast belief and positive thinking have always got him back from grave medical situations. She has been the prime mover in his academic success where he has cleared his 12th standard.

Sumithra's workshops on sustenance models aren't limited to the community. She walks the talk. Sai Bakery is a neighbourhood initiative set up by Sumithra to provide a sense of purpose for our son. She steadfastly evangelized the habitat to accept a set of adults with special needs to run a business model from home. Each individual was empowered and assigned a role. They were made to work as a team. Resources were tapped to create business. And today, the Sai Bakery team knows how to leverage their capabilities rather than languish on perceived shortcomings.

We should cut to another flashback here, our courting days again. Sumithra and I were seated in a temple. Amidst the chants of Lord Shiva that could be heard faintly in the background and intermittent sound of bells, she narrated her growing up years.

As a child, she had varied opinions about herself – good, bad, naughty, impish, funny, chirpy and completely effervescent. She talked me through her troubled childhood, misplaced aggression and time of regression in school. Her hyperactive self was always misunderstood for having a lack of clarity and focus in life. At the brink of degeneration, she stumbled upon her calling that led her through a phase of realization, which in her words put her firmly on the road to redemption. She turned her angst and belligerence in gaining knowledge and evolving into a multitasking, multifaceted, extremely talented person capable of forcing change in diverse sectors.

I believe her immense courage and a certain kind of distinctive smartness were honed during those tough years. Talking about her courage, I recall the day a few pavement dwellers had come home asking for Sumithra's help. We were in Mumbai at that time and a girl among them had caused a bloody feud between two groups. It was no surprise that Sumithra took up the issue, made a feisty entry, resolved the situation and got the girl married to a suitor from the opposite group. A year later, the couple visited us with their daughter whom they had named Sumithra.

As I write this, I comprehend the innumerable things I have learned from her. I remember the day she spoke to me about transgender people and their lives. She had worked on a documentary to capture their travails. So these days when a eunuch comes up asking for alms at a traffic signal, I have the empathy hand over some money with a smile.

The manifold ways in which she positively influences the lives of people around her is best represented by the feedback of Colonel RVVS Jagati from Awanitpore Air Force Base (Jammu & Kashmir). He writes, "The workshop gave a new dimension to the very thought process of oneself. It was quite thought-provoking. It gave a reason to look into the inner self and carry out a candid study of the own being."

On the same lines of Sumithra's ability to touch people's inner lives, Chennai-based IT professional Krishna Raj writes, "I first met her as a Hostess in Sadya 2010 – a fund raising event for VidyaSagar Special School and right from that moment I have never seen her energy level down. Many aspire to do something for the society but very few actually do that and inspire others to be socially responsible. She showed me the way and inspires many like me in the corporate world to reach out – that's our ever energetic Smyta."

Smyta is Sumithra's maiden name, which some still prefer. The Tamil version of the name it spelt as 'Sumaitha', which means asking to carry or bear another's weight.

Social consciousness and the quest to create a responsible society have not smothered Sumithra's zest for life. In a day filled with counselling, travelling to places resolving real-life problems, fighting for inclusion and making documentaries, she also makes time to turn up for a social get-together, infusing life and sparkle. She's a gorgeous dancer, seasoned singer and appreciates art in any form. She always is the star in any wedding album in the family. An excellent cook, she never misses an opportunity to pleasantly surprise us with native and international cuisines. Another trait of her is to never waste. She can bring together totally distant leftovers to create a delicacy that's sought after.

This quality of being a rockstar activist makes her an icon the youth want to emulate. Sumithra is arguably the busiest activist on Facebook. Leveraging the reach of social platforms, she uses them as a powerful mode of communication to create awareness and muster support. Immediately after reading one of her posts, a bright banker from Dubai, Faiz Affandi, called to say, "Madam, I need to transfer the money required to fund a month's medicine for the woman battling cancer. I read your post on Facebook and with no second thought felt that I need to help this woman who's also the mother of a special child."

As I turn around, my eyes fall on our daughter Saujanya, who is communicating in fluent sign language to a bunch of hearing-impaired students. I can't help but feel proud for a child like her to have made the effort to pick up the language at such a tender age. No points for guessing the influence and the reason she intuitively feels for people and the need to help them.

Next, I spot the citations placed on the wall. It says, "Sumithra Prasad has dedicated her life to selfless social service despite facing seemingly insurmountable personal challenges – lifelong fight for social justice through citizen action, Karamveer Puraskaar 2010."

Another appreciation reads as, "The award is a token of grateful appreciation of the entire society for the meritorious work". It also adds, "She had proved to be a role model for skillfully meeting the challenges presented by life and emerging as a true leader in promoting social awareness – Sadguru Gnanananda Award, 2009."

How very appropriate!

There are innumerable young ones who love to call Sumithra their mother. There are youngsters who are proud to have her as their mentor. Once shy, today they dismount their bikes when they see an inebriated soul lying on the road. Holding the man by his dirty shirt, they pull him to the pavement without judging. These are also those individuals who are learning to be more patient with their elders and be more responsible towards the society. Then there are peers who, without hesitation, consider her an inspiration, elderly who consider her as their sunshine girl. A post on her Facebook wall written by an elderly gentleman, 78-year-old holistic healer Lakshman Iyer from Chennai, reads, "*Su Mithra* means excellent, good friend, and you are that always, anywhere and everywhere in the universe."

Sectors, individuals and sections of society draw courage from Sumithra's strength. Entities continue to leverage her experience for creating a better world.

Sectors, individuals and sections of society draw courage from Sumithra's strength. Entities continue to leverage her experience for creating a better world. Distressed know that help or support is just a call away. Different bodies believing in her are bestowing awards as recognition of her service, like the much appreciated Mother Teresa Award for selfless service.

For Sumithra, barriers are meant to be broken. Neither distance nor ethnicity could pose a problem. From far-flung villages in the south to remote terrains in the north, she has travelled the distance. Be it the bustling metros or secluded spreads of the West, she has fought and won many a battles that positively influenced the community.

Children, adolescents, young adults, grown-ups and elderly – Sumithra has been a charismatic agent of change who holds appeal for everyone. It has been possible because of her unique ability to look at the world through the eyes of others and also enrich them by layering her experience and wisdom.

Sumithra has been treading greatness as if it's normal. She now knows that the road walked upon so far has been rightly laid down with a reason. The twists and turns in her life have culminated in bringing her deeper understanding, thereby launching her into a path of profundity. Yet she says, "The woods are deep and the distance too far. Many more miles to go till I can sleep…"

Like any person who's completely in sync with their purpose in this world, Sumithra's walk of life continues unabated.

Biographer

Rajendra J. Prasad is Sumithra Prasad's husband. He is a business head working with MEC, a leading communications planning agency. Not limited to the role of being Sumithra Prasad's biggest fan, he also helps her from behind the scenes, by giving her the support she requires. He is a steadfast believer in her capabilities and an omnipresent ally in her journey.

moJOsh Inspirator Power 17:
The Power of Compassion
(Includes Kindness)

"Be kind, for everyone you meet is fighting a harder battle."

~ Plato

Thought Leadership for Reflection: Compassion means empathic feelings, sensitivity, emotions and concern for the sufferings or misfortunes of others. The *Bhagavad Gita* and other holy books say consciousness is understanding the suffering of others without it happening to ourselves. How? Because we are all connected. We are all ONE.

Ideas for Action: Take five minutes every day to be kind and compassionate towards our fellow beings and also animals. You could simply message a joke to someone who is feeling under the weather. You could simply smile at a person in an elevator and brighten their day. You could simply connect two people who may have potential synergies to collaborate and do something together.

18

Spreading the Light
Tulasi Munda

Tulsi Munda was born exactly a month before India got her independence from the British in 1947. Very early in life, this poor Adivasi girl from one of the most backward regions of Orissa began exhibiting her love for independence and unconventional way of thinking. She grew up with her own notions of freedom and slavery – notions that were strikingly different from the beliefs held by the people in her milieu. While other children played, tended goats in the fields or worked in the iron-ore mines, Tulsi wanted to study. She wanted to educate herself, learn new things and speak exciting languages like Hindi and English. Instead, she sat at home and helped her widowed mother with housework. Her four sisters and two brothers went out to work. She, being the youngest, stayed home.

Tulsi yearned to study, but it was a futile desire. There was no school in their village, Painsi. In any case, nobody in the area educated their girls. When she was 12, she went to live with her sister in Serenda, a village 65 km away. She earned ₹2 a week by cutting stones, sifting iron from the waste. Whenever she could, she taught herself the alphabets. It was difficult, but she plodded on.

In 1961, her passion for learning catapulted her into the orbit of women like Malti Chaudhury, Roma Devi and Nirmala Deshpande, renowned personalities committed to social work, especially that of educating women. She joined them and participated in their village forays and struggles in different parts of the country. She met Vinobha Bhave and was inspired by his vision and commitment to donate land (Bhoodan Movement) and improve the lives of poor villagers.

It was in 1964 that Tulsi she returned to Serenda. Her mission in life was clear. A victim of illiteracy, she would dedicate her life to eradicating this scourge. She resolved, "As long as I have breath in my body, I will fight illiteracy." She would devote herself to teaching and educating children, especially girls. Illiteracy, she believed, was the worst form of enslavement. It was the root cause of the evils she saw all around her – poverty, unemployment, alcoholism, superstition and fear. Education was the tool to free people's minds from the darkness of ignorance. But executing her mission proved to be tougher than she had anticipated.

Villagers found the concept of educating girls preposterous, and boys had to work in the fields and mines to earn money, not waste their time learning alphabets and numbers and alien languages like English and Hindi.

Villagers found the concept of educating girls preposterous, and boys had to work in the fields and mines to earn money, not waste their time learning alphabets and numbers and alien languages like English and Hindi. But Tusli Munda was undeterred, even though she had neither students nor a venue for that matter. She persuaded Serenda's local *pradhan* to allow her to use his verandah for a few hours. As children could not be spared during the day, she started teaching evening classes.

The trickle began. Before Tulsi knew it, she had 30 children. She taught them the basics: just alphabets and numbers and a smattering of English words. She says, "Even if he (the student) grew up to be a driver, a few words of English would help him to get a better job in Bhubaneshwar or even Kolkata."

Tulsi taught in the evenings and attended to *bhoodan* work during the day. But soon, her school began to take up more and more of her time. Villagers, who worked all day long, began sending their small children to Tulsi's verandah. They treated it like a crèche, but Tulsi didn't mind. Even three-year-olds were welcome. Some children were spending the whole day with her. The verandah got too small. So in 1966, she shifted her school to a plot of land with a shed, a little distance away. It was almost outside the village. Dense with trees and shrubs and sparsely populated, the children were, at first, afraid to come to their new school. But Tulsi was fearless. She spent the night all alone in this wilderness. "I was doing God's work, why should I worry? I had a picture of Rama and Krishna and soon the children realized that I had God's protection," recalls Tulsi.

Tulsi went on to spend the rest of her life there. As there was only one tin shed where she slept at night, she began by teaching the children under a tree. It is a tribute to her indomitable will and indefatigable energy that over the next 40 years, Tulsi helped establish 17 schools and succeeded in educating 20,000 boys and girls. Currently, she has over 500 students, almost half of whom are girls and her school provides education all the way up to Class X.

Biographer

Anita Pratap is a Karamveer Puraskaar award recipient, and is an expatriate Indian writer and journalist. In 1983, she was the first journalist who interviewed LTTE chief V. Prabhakaran. She won the George Polk Award for television reporting of the takeover of Kabul by the Taliban. She was also the India bureau chief of CNN.

moJOsh Inspirator Power 18:
The Power of Purpose
(Includes Spiritual Health)

"You cannot invent your purpose, you discover and detect it."

~ Dr. Viktor Frankl

Thought Leadership for Reflection: Purpose is the reason for which something is done or created, or for which something exists. It's also a person's sense of resolve or determination. What is the reason for our existence? Most people run through life without knowing where they are going. They have never figured their purpose and hence don't know which direction they want to go in. Therefore, the human race has been reduced to the rat race.

Ideas for Action: Simply write your mission statement with integrity (also called the statement of purpose and remember, you are not doing this to fudge your way into an Ivy League institute, you doing this for yourself, so be true because you can never ever lie to only one person and that person is you) to make real your deepest desires, dreams, aspirations for 15 minutes and let the pen flow. You will be amazed how the thoughts flow. Every week (every day, if possible), revisit and refine your mission statement. Refer to inspirational mission statements on the internet and get inspired by those thoughts.

*While writing your mission statement you may play some soothing music of your choice to calm your mind and focus better.

19

Finding Her Footing

Vandana Shah

With a paltry sum of ₹750, the *bahu* of a respected family was out on the streets at about 2 am, with nothing but tears and bewilderment at the cruelty of her new-found family, her dreams and the grit to survive. She said to herself: "I must amount to something in life. No one will ever trample upon me again, because I will be a 'somebody'."

When Vandana Shah recounts her story, her eyes blaze with conviction, one can't miss the steely resolve evident on her face. And the 'something' that this 'somebody' eventually did, even after life dealt her with severe stifling blows, has not only turned her own life around (a full 360 degree!) but has helped hundreds of other women in similar predicaments seek a new identity and meaning in life. Through her path-breaking book on divorce and her divorce support group, Vandana, perhaps unknown to even herself, set about challenging the mores of a patriarchal middle-class society that obviously has different rules and expectations for women and men. Her objective in life: to make 'divorce' sound a less dirty word than it is, even today, never mind the laws and changed mindsets. In other words, she wants to reduce the stigma of divorce, provide non-judgmental support to those going through it and, above all, rebuild a life while going through this in India – a country where we have almost no support groups or even progressive laws in place for those going through a divorce.

Vandana, a youthful *Mumbaikar*, might be a writer, activist, a Lead India finalist, a lawyer, environmentalist and a feminist – but over and above all of these, she is a girl (and I deliberately describe her as a 'girl') who knows how to have fun. Perhaps it is this unique quality that separates her from most other women. 'Vandy' has this ability to retain her sense of humour even in the face of the most adverse situations. It doesn't mean that she doesn't take them seriously or get bogged down at times. But she believes in facing problems chin up and going full steam ahead instead of brooding over them and making herself feel more miserable. Her philosophy: "I learnt to look at the positive side of situations because I am an orphan and if you are sad all the time no one wants to be with you over an extended period of time. It's better to look at life half-full," says she. It is a cliché she has internalized well, over the years.

Besides, she says, "Life is too short. My parents died when they were in their 60s, so I want to experience every bit of life with unadulterated joy."

Vandana's positivity is perhaps inherited. She was born in a family where her father, Wing Commander Sanwal Shah, was a decorated Indian Air Force pilot. Having fought three wars, he used to assuage his wife's fears about going into battle by saying, "Don't worry, only two things can happen to me – either I'll live or die. Nothing more." Vandana's mother was a housewife who devoted her time to looking after her family.

Vandana's first blow came in her early 20s when she lost both her parents to cancer. Being orphaned at an early age did bring its own share of grief, but she continued her education, exploring her talent and discovering life. After a few years, the familiar pressure started – of getting married and settling down in a 'good' family.

She thought she had it all when she finally met her Prince Charming – a scion of a rich, renowned family. It was an arranged marriage and the biggest honour bestowed upon her at that point in time was that he had seen ("inspected") over 200 girls before choosing to marry her.

Unfortunately, it didn't take long for all her hopes to bite the dust. The love and romance that she had expected were expressed in the form of bruises on her back and face. The praises for her beauty and intelligence showered on her in public turned to abuses in private.

Her new family didn't want Vandana. They wanted a certain image of the ideal daughter-in-law and when she didn't conform or fit into it, the abuse and violence started.

She did put up with it for a long time. After all, aren't all good Indian girls supposed to adjust and take the blame? The intense fear and shame associated with even thinking about divorce had her making a go at her marriage at any cost, right from agreeing to see a counsellor to even agreeing to signing apology letters on stamp papers.

And then came the night that changed it all. After a particularly bad bout of vitriolic abuse, she was thrown out of her marital home with a mere ₹750 in hand. It was the moment when push came to shove – literally and figuratively. The *bahu* of a respected family was out on the streets with nothing. But even as she stood with tears streaking her cheeks,

> "I learnt to look at the positive side of situations because I am an orphan and if you are sad all the time no one wants to be with you over an extended period of time."
> ~ Vandana Shah

she thought, "I may have lost everything, but my dreams are alive and look at me, I AM ALIVE. That alone makes me a billionaire."

An intense period of tears, confusion and soul searching followed, and Vandana realized that, leave alone material wealth, all she had was hope, belief and a will to survive.

That single event led Vandana to think that there must be thousands of women like her who were in a similar position, and many of them, perhaps even worse off than her. She had to reclaim her life and what better way to do it than seek help and guide others?

The first step was forming a support group for divorced, abused and separated women called 360 Degrees Back To Life. The name couldn't have been more apt. After all, a divorce in traditional Indian society meant 'closure' in some ways and a woman had to literally start from scratch, building her emotional, financial and social support system. That learning was a 360-degree cycle, and then once that cycle was over, a new phase of life started.

The group was also open to men, because men really have no recourse to any emotional support. The idea behind starting the group was to provide non-judgemental support to those going through a divorce, and 360 Degrees Back To Life turned out to be India's first such group that provided a positive perspective to rebuilding lives even while going through a relationship breakdown.

Simultaneously, Vandana decided to fight for justice – her own divorce battle. It turned out to be a long, tumultuous, frustrating affair that was to end only after nearly a decade. Each hearing was painful with Vandana having to put up with the litany of lawyers and their changing stances, the mounting expenses of fighting what seemed to be a futile case, the taunts of an unforgiving society and the sheer vulnerability of being an almost single woman. She was fighting a rather powerful adversary – her powerful in-laws and their connections. Not surprisingly, the divorce case turned uglier by the year, charges were traded with character assassination in full swing. Any other woman would have cowed down, but Vandana, with the support of her friends, well-wishers and her group members, kept on fighting. Though, surprisingly, her real family of sisters and other relatives chose to shut their doors and hearts to her. The ill-effect of the court case, amongst others: her growing girth, as she often self-depreciatingly quips!

However, those were also the years when she realized another truth that went on to govern her life: "You can forget your pain if you help others overcome theirs."

With that, Vandana's energies were spent in making the support group move from strength to strength. Counselling others made her realize that problems like loneliness, facing sexual innuendos at work and unstable finances are universal issues to be faced in the journey of divorce. This led to the next milestone in her life – a book based on her own experiences as well as of her support group members. The book was titled *360 Degrees Back To Life – A Litigant's Humorous Perspective on Divorce*, and was endorsed by the iconic feminist, Gloria Steinem.

Unlike the existing write-ups on the topic of divorce, Vandana decided to take a lighter look at the entire issue, offering advice and even handy tips on handling the drama that follows. The book fetched her lot of recognition. Not only was it covered extensively by the local and international media, it even impacted others' lives. Even today, she gets urgent emails asking for the book and her expert advice.

The book was launched in India by none other than lyricist Javed Akhtar, who lauded Vandana's efforts and said, "It is only the courageous that can look with humour at the black areas of their life." There have been knowledge sessions around the book at the US Consulate and the UK High Commission along with interactive panel discussions. It was even launched in Oman in the international market.

In due course, even as she was keeping her dates with her divorce hearing on the side, Vandana's conviction 'of elevating her own life instead of bringing down the other' started gaining currency. She was one of the finalists, selected among over a 100,000 people, for the Lead India campaign initiated by The Times of India Group to select leaders for the future. She also got involved in a non-governmental organization (NGO) that promoted a United Nations-endorsed technique of environmental management. Additionally, she attended various global summits for the empowerment of women and one such interaction led her to meet Gloria Steinem. Each meeting, every seminar and each counselling session provided a healing touch to her own problems. Gradually, she became stronger as a person, ready to face anything that life threw at her.

A very brave aspect of the book was that it was extremely truthful and Vandana had exposed her life – warts and all – and had hidden nothing from anyone, for as she said in her own words, "If you want others to benefit from your experiences, then you must be honest." She often jokes, "I'd be the worst candidate for blackmail as all my life stories are out in the public for everyone to read."

Counselling others made her realize that problems like loneliness, facing sexual innuendos at work and unstable finances are universal issues to be faced in the journey of divorce.

Another important thing that happened to Vandana was that she wrote the book whilst the case was still going on. Thus, in effect, the healing and detachment had already taken place while the horrific events in her life were still unfolding. This is usually not the case as most people are forced to experience closure before healing.

The support group might have led Vandana to discover her hitherto unexplored talent for writing, but the change that it brought in her life was more internal than external. The positive philosophy of the group helped her transform many lives. It gave hope to women who often felt that divorce had taken their lives away from them. They felt that they had a chance to rebuild it all over again. The main thrust of Vandana's group was to cope with challenges of separation by focusing on the strengths rather than the weaknesses. Cutting across socio-economic barriers, women identified what their needs were and shared legal, moral and sometimes, economic support. The result was that it changed the lives of over 10,000 people in one-on-one counselling, group sessions and via emails. Of course, the chain of change keeps spreading through the healed members themselves, and though the problems are immense, the 'can do' spirit that defines Vandana is being shared by her group members as well.

The group has done this for gratis for over a decade; as Vandana says, "The best payment is a life saved." However, during all these years, her own divorce drama had been showing no signs of abating. Plus the need to keep the group alive on limited resources was constantly playing on her mind. But she never gave up. On the contrary, humour was her weapon even in the most trying circumstances. The stress of a tough battle in court was showing in her quick weight gain, but rather than getting disappointed with it, she learnt to laugh at herself. If she faced a wicked taunt, she would give it back, tit for tat, tongue firmly in cheek. Slowly, she was inching towards her goal to develop her own identity, sans the suffix of a powerful married surname.

Finally, her divorce came through after a period of nearly ten years and Vandana was free. The decade had taken a toll but it had also enriched her in many ways. It had made her even more determined to help others in similar situations and she joined a law college to become a fully trained lawyer. The basic idea was to understand the nuances of law better and not let litigants get taken for a ride by lawyers.

Post her divorce, Vandana decided to take her mission of helping divorcees further. And that's when she embarked on a new project – a first-of-its-kind news magazine on divorce called *ExFiles*. It started as a simple news magazine that covered all aspects of divorce. Though it was a staggering effort due to money constraints, the response was overwhelming. The magazine was distributed in the family court in Bandra, Mumbai, and the moment it hit the stands, Vandana was flooded with enquiries from people seeking counselling – all of which once again highlighted the huge lacuna that exists in this field in India.

Then came the book, *Ex Files,* which was published by Penguin under the Shobhaa De imprint. This book was endorsed by Padma Vibhushan Dr. Sonal Mansingh and

Padma Bhushan Lord Meghnad Desai, and has become a bestseller. *Ex Files* has been now made a part of the law colleges in some cities in India and was launched by the Attorney General of India Mukul Rohatgi and also the Chief Justice of Bombay High Court, Mohit Shah.

All these efforts have completed an entire cycle for Vandana. She has identified that her life's mission is to help others who had suffered the way she did. Legally and socially, she says, she wants to provide a complete safety net.

But in many ways, Vandana's journey has just begun. Her goals for the future are clear in her mind – to increase the activities of the group by increasing its presence in more places in India, and to have alliances with production houses for documentaries and talk shows based on the problem of divorce in India.

Through it all, she also discovered her true calling – writing. The first book was perhaps an emotional outpouring resulting from a burning need to express her thoughts, challenges and frustrations. But the response to the book and the subsequent events led Vandana to realize that words were her weapons that would help her initiate a change. She has turned into a columnist for *The Huffington Post* as well as *Dainik Bhaskar*. Her words also appear in *Savvy*, *Thrive* (Arianna Huffington's new venture) and *Black and White*, a publication from Oman. This, coupled with her circumstances, led her to study and practice law in the family court in Mumbai. Currently, her hands are full with high-profile divorce cases.

Vandana's efforts gained international recognition when the *BBC* made a documentary featuring her work. It was broadcasted on the International Women's Day. She was also interviewed by the *BBC* on law and the divorce scene in India. Vandana continues to be quoted by national and international publications as an expert on the subject.

Besides all this, the accolades keep coming. She has been awarded the Best Lawyer in India and her work as a social entrepreneur got recognition when she was awarded the Karamveer Puraskaar at Rajghat. This has spurred her decision to dedicate the rest of her life to women's empowerment and making a difference. She wants to live up to the promise she had made to herself on that dark night, with just dreams in her eyes and a meagre amount of ₹750 in her pocket.

Vandana says, "I will rebuild my life by elevating myself rather than pulling down another."

It looks like there will be yet another twist to the 360-degree turn and let's see where that thrilling adventure goes...

Biographer

Lekha Menon is a journalist with over 15 years of experience and the editor of *Masala!*, the most popular Asian lifestyle magazine in the UAE. Prior to her stint in Dubai, she has worked with *Mumbai Mirror, The Times of India, DNA* and *Hindustan Times.*

moJOsh Inspirator Power 19:
The Power of Leadership
(Includes Perspective)

"Leaders become great not because of their own power, but because of their ability to empower others."

~ John Maxwell

Thought Leadership for Reflection: Over the years, the concept of leadership has got much convoluted. People are given to believe that leaders have followers, or leaders lead teams and organizations, or leaders know everything. The truth is that real leaders have no such arrogance and relate with others from a space of humility and vulnerability. We must remember there are no born leaders, because leadership is an acquired skill in order to practice human values and inspire others to bring out the best in them.

Ideas for Action: As a leader, you have the integrity to bring out the best in people and help them to see their real value, their self-worthiness, the true potential and power that they may not have seen in themselves. You coach them to unleash their optimum potential and discover their true powers. You listen; you understand their challenges and then help them to find their own solutions to their challenges. You do not feel you are better or superior to others and consider yourself as one amongst equals.

20

Keeping the Deccan Alive

Vijayanath Shenoy

Vijayanath Shenoy is a collector. But the word 'collector' conjures up visions of a snob who is rich, urbane, and possibly even pretentious. But Vijayanath is down-to-earth, simple and genuine. Though a natural aesthete, he never set out to be a collector. He just became one, unconsciously but inexorably. He reveals rather cryptically, "Being a collector is a source of negative pleasure for me. I was only relieving my pain caused by the wanton destruction of our heritage."

Vijayanath collects old homes – beautiful, intricately carved, ancestral homes that belonged to the wealthy landed gentry of South Karnataka. Land reforms, modernization and urbanization that broke down joint family systems and pastoral livelihoods began to erode a way of life that had existed for centuries. Unwanted by their city dwelling heirs, ancestral homes – empty or inhabited by aging grandparents – began collapsing in the countryside. Piled high on carts, exquisitely carved wooden ceilings, pillars and doors made their final journey to the slaughter house of saw mills to be sliced and sold as firewood. Lovingly sculpted bell metal objects were melted down in foundries.

Vijayanath watched and grieved. He could not bear to see the annihilation of his homeland's traditional architecture. These homes were not mere mud and wood edifices. He explains, "Architecture is the most visible symbol of our cultural heritage. Music and dance are powerful, but not tangible the way buildings are. These homes represented the conceptualization of our ethos, the imagination of our

ancestors, the ingenious indigenous technology and the
skill of native craftsmen. They provide cultural continuity.
They connect us with our heritage. But the connection was
breaking; our heritage was disappearing. And with that,
our sense of identity would be lost too. Soon, there will be
nothing left to link us to our roots. I *had* to step in to save
these homes."

That was in the 1974 and as an employee of Syndicate Bank
in Manipal, 40-year-old Vijayanath Shenoy did not have much
money to undertake his mission. So he began by rescuing a
door here, a pillar there, from the brutal encounter with the
buzz saw. He bought what he could afford. What he couldn't,
he pleaded with the owners to donate to him instead of selling
to scrap dealers. He retrieved traditional artifacts from junk
yards, unused attics and debris of demolished homes. Bit by
bit, he collected and built a home for himself using all these
salvaged materials.

It took him five years to complete the house he named
Hasta Shilpa – Creation by Hand. It was not merely a
museum of traditional craft; it was a condensed recreation
of a composite architectural tradition in all its glory. It
conformed to the principles of *Vastu Shastra*, which combines
physics with metaphysics, utility with harmony. Above all, it
was a monumental vision of loveliness – a memory coming
alive from the past to touch the soul of the visitors. The
fabled beauty of this recreated home spread far and wide.
Intellectuals, commoners, students all flocked to Manipal
to marvel the house that Vijayanath had built. It touched
a powerful chord in the public. But it struck a discordant
note at home. It became impossible for the Shenoy family to
live in a house where visitors streamed in constantly. His two
children could not study. His wife had no privacy. The choice
was stark: either they ban visitors or they move out. Vijayanath
did not agonize over the decision. In 1991, he converted
Hasta Shilpa into a public charitable trust and moved out to
a new and ordinary home. Hasta Shilpa contained priceless

objects, but there was no question of selling the house because he fervently believed he was not the 'owner'; he was merely its custodian. Heritage is not a matter of individual ownership; it is an issue of collective entitlement. How could he change track and become selfish when it was this belief that had spurred him on his mission?

Vijayanath vividly recalls the pain of seeing a beautiful ancestral home in Malnad being torn down by its owner in 1983. He begged, pleaded and cajoled, but the adamant owner only got angrier. In desperation, Vijayanath yelled at him, "You have no right to demolish this house. It doesn't belong to you. It belongs to all of us." The owner got so furious at Vijayanath's effrontery that he had him physically thrown out of his estate. From a distance, Vijayanath watched the grand old manor come down. He wept for the second time in his life. The first was when his mother died. Two decades have gone by, but the memory remains an unhealed wound. Vijayanath's voice breaks and his blazing eyes fill with unshed tears as he remembers the humbling of a glorious tradition.

> "Architecture is the most visible symbol of our cultural heritage. Music and dance are powerful, but not tangible the way buildings are."
> ~ Vijayanath Shenoy

From that helplessness was born a steely determination to save not only homes, but the precious architectural heritage of his region. It was not enough to save a few utensils, window frames and carved doors. He had to save whole homes that contained within its shaded interiors, the whispering narratives of his ancestors. From an ordinary bank employee, he became an extraordinary heritage conservationist. A new vision possessed him – to set up a heritage village in Manipal where he could transplant and preserve whole homes. It was a difficult and delicate task – dismantling crumbling homes, transporting every little item, reassembling and preserving them.

With ₹40 lakh donation from NORAD, the Norwegian aid agency, and six acres of land from the government, Vijayanath dedicated himself to fulfilling his vision. He now has reassembled 26 beautiful traditional structures in his heritage village. The buildings represent different architectural styles, both secular and sacred. It comprises hermitages, temples and homes belonging to Brahmins, Mangalorean Christians and Nizams, to affluent feudal landlords and even an ascetic Hindu pontiff.

What is perhaps most striking about these gracious old homes is the way they arise naturally from the womb of the earth. What imbues them with this aura of belonging to the local context, of oneness with the surrounding nature is perhaps the fact that the building materials are natural and drawn from the nearby forests, plains, sea coasts and rivers. The houses are built with timber, granite, laterite, terracotta tiles, mud, limestone, straw and sand – all biodegradable. They came from the earth and unto the earth they shall return. These are unlike the modern reinforced concrete cement (RCC) monstrosities that have disfigured the countryside.

Modernity is useful and inevitable, but Vijayanath feels it should not come at the price of sacrificing tradition.

Vijayanath hates them with a passion. He exclaims, "These RCC structures are like cancer. The earth won't take them back. They are more dangerous than nuclear bombs. When I see an RCC construction, I feel like reaching out for a hand grenade." He acknowledges that modern skyscrapers need to be built of glass and chrome, steel and cement. But he doesn't understand why people use RCC to build matchboxes they call homes, which trap heat, to cope with which they need air conditioners that punish them with huge electricity bills.

Modernity is useful and inevitable, but Vijayanath feels it should not come at the price of sacrificing tradition. A deeply cultured man, Vijayanath loves traditional art, dance, music, theatre, literature and sculpture. In 1961, he set up Sangeet Sabha in Manipal to promote Indian classical music and dance. His initiatives resulted in all the living legends of Indian traditional art forms to visit Manipal and give live performances and talks.

Vijayanath's passions, loves and compulsions are coded in his DNA. They stir his soul, flow in his veins. An enduring philosophical conundrum is whether man makes history or whether history finds the right person at the right time to create history. Vijayanath believes history finds the man. "Nature chooses her champions," he says, adding, "All around me, heritage was being destroyed. Heritage needed to be saved and it found me."

Vijayanath Shenoy's Heritage Village is not open to tourists. It is only for the discerning visitors – students of architecture, scholars, researchers, designers and conservationists. Vijayanath asserts, "It is a kind of university, not Disneyland to which busloads of beer drinking tourists come to gape and entertain themselves." With its array of elaborately handcrafted homes, its stunning galleries of historic Ravi Varma lithographs and magnificent Tanjore paintings, its museum of tribal sculptures, folk and contemporary art, it's training centre for artisans to keep alive traditional skills in handloom weaving, pottery, metal casting, wood carving, mud processing and stone cutting, the Heritage Village is a tribute to the vision and will of one remarkable man. Posterity has to be eternally grateful to Vijayanath for single-handedly conserving South Karnataka's rich architectural legacy. His success demonstrates how passionate dedication driven by noble, unselfish motives can achieve spectacular results.

But Vijayanath doesn't see it that way. He says: "Only pain will drive you to succeed. If you experience intense pain, then every action of yours becomes part of your struggle to relieve pain. In that process, you succeed. But it is not the worldly success that motivates you. It is the desire to vanquish pain."

Pain drove Vijayanath Shenoy to save his heritage, and Deccan architectural heritage found its champion and saviour.

Biographer

Anita Pratap is a Karamveer Puraskaar award recipient, and is an expatriate Indian writer and journalist. In 1983, she was the first journalist who interviewed LTTE chief V. Prabhakaran. She won the George Polk Award for television reporting of the takeover of Kabul by the Taliban. She was also the India bureau chief of CNN.

moJOsh Inspirator Power 20:
The Power of Fairness
(Includes Informed Judgment and Forgiveness)

"Being good is easy, what is difficult is being just and fair."

~ Victor Hugo

Thought Leadership for Reflection: I always joke in a light-hearted manner, with people who attend my speeches and learning programmes around the world, that the concept of fairness in our world today has been reduced to facial fairness, body fairness, armpit fairness and even fairness creams for intimate body parts. Jokes aside, a win-win mindset and treating people with fairness is slowly but surely becoming extinct in our world.

Ideas for action: We must learn to treat everyone fairly and have a win-win mindset in all our relationships. The give and take should always be balanced with equal courage and consideration so that the benefits are mutual and thus respect and trust is mutual and sustainable in all relationships. We should not be hasty to judge people without clarifying and understanding their situation and should have the integrity to forgive people for mistakes they make, after helping them to learn from the mistake so that it is not repeated.

21

The Irresistible Rise of the Pomegranate Kid

Villoo Morawala-Patell

Villoo Morawala-Patell is a maverick. She just doesn't fit the image people have of leaders of either the scientific fraternity or the business community. Too brash, too pushy, too presumptuous, too exuberant, too young, too quick, too this, too that... She is also, quite simply, brilliant.

I first met Villoo in mid-1989 when I arrived in India to take up a job with International Crops Research Institute for the Semi-Arid Tropics (ICRISAT), an international agricultural research centre in Hyderabad. She was already there, and had been for a decade, working as a research scholar with Tetsuo Matsumoto, a Japanese scientist, as well as John Peacock and many other Indian and global biochemists, physiologists and plant breeders.

She quickly befriended many of us foreigners, and along with several others, I got invited to the *navjot* ceremony of her younger daughter Sanaya. Judging this an opportunity to get to know something new about this amazing country, I brought along my young son Tucker, who, like Sanaya, was six years old. Little did anyone know that 21 years later, our two families would again meet at another Parsi ceremony, but more about that later.

Villoo left Hyderabad in October of that year and I forgot about her. But she was back three-and-a-half years later, festooned with a brand new PhD from the University of Strasbourg in France. She immediately began to stir things up. She visited ICRISAT and bombarded the management with startling ideas about developing a public-private biotech company on the campus. Without pausing for breath, she rattled off a list of laboratory equipment she needed and where to set them up. This was too much for a corporate culture that in the mid-90s still mirrored the traditions of hierarchy and seniority that typified the Indian civil service. Moreover, the thinking was that international research should be conducted in a cocoon, sheltered from the crass demands and result-based thinking of the business world. All this was to change dramatically later, and today ICRISAT hosts a wide array of public and private partners on its vast campus at Patancheru. But in 1993, Villoo was in no mind to wait. She had bigger fish to fry.

Villoo looked around for potential partners and sponsors in Hyderabad, but soon lost patience with the overly cautious climate she encountered. People were reluctant to accept things they couldn't understand, like biotechnology and aggressive female scientists. Academics were busy re-inventing wheels and business had no budget for research and development. So when Hyderabad proved too small for this strident young scientist with her boundless energy and wild ideas, she took off for Bangalore, where she reckoned she'd have a better chance to flourish.

People were reluctant to accept things they couldn't understand, like biotechnology and aggressive female scientists.

She was right. Although Bangalore mirrored the rest of India in many respects, the pulse there was faster than elsewhere. After some searching around, Villoo managed to find space in the labs of the National Centre for Biological Sciences (NCBS) on the campus of the Indian Institute of Science, thanks to Prof. K.Vijay Raghavan and Prof. Obaid Siddiqui, who gave her the two bench spots and a roof from where she could make a start. She gathered a small team, and without pausing to breathe began to undertake groundbreaking work in biotechnology. She caught the eye of the Rockefeller Foundation, which was actively seeking to support young Indian scientists who were likely to stay in the country to help build a strong scientific infrastructure. The foundation's assistance and that of Dr. Richard Jefferson was valuable and allowed Villoo to build a strong team, but it wasn't long before she once again ran out of elbow room. NCBS suggested she might be better served at the University of Agricultural Sciences (UAS), also in Bangalore.

She booked an appointment with the vice-chancellor of UAS, Prof. G.K. Veeresh. Here's what ensued in Villoo's own words: "I went to see the vice-chancellor with an unripe pomegranate. I gave it to him and told him, 'I have brought you this gift. An unripe pomegranate. I need a place to be nurtured and grown, to become a multi-seeded fruit, and for that, I need your help. Please give me some space.'"

Prof. Veeresh, a bit of a maverick himself, looked Villoo in the eye and saw something smouldering deep inside. Here was someone who would not sit still, someone who would make a difference, a pomegranate that needed only a bit of nurturing. He, along with Prof. Uday Kumar, told her that although accommodating her through normal channels was difficult for political reasons, and offered her a Professor Emeritus, a designation that would provide her with lab space. So here she was, a Professor Emeritus at the ripe old age of 43!

The Pomegranate Kid was off to Europe a couple of instances during this time and I again lost track of her. By the time she flew across my radar screen again, I had left ICRISAT and started a consulting firm specializing in science writing and photojournalism. One of my clients was the Rockefeller Foundation. They wanted me to write about India's National Rice Biotechnology Network, which they had supported for several years. They were winding down their support and wanted some sort of publication that traced the network's history – its trials, tribulations and successes. I accepted the assignment, travelling the length and breadth of India to find out the where, and when and who of rice biotechnology. In doing so, I couldn't avoid bumping into that cauldron of energy that resembled a pomegranate. She was very grateful to Rockefeller and was delighted to be interviewed for the publication, especially by an old friend. I did the interview, took a few photos of her team and went back to Hyderabad to finish the book. But something she had said stuck in my mind.

Villoo had said something about a new company, a biotech firm that would be based in Bangalore, and that would have a public agenda as well as a commercial one. She had been saying the same kind of thing for years and no one had taken her seriously. But her tone had been different this time – more confident, more self-assured. I asked my scientist friends about her. It was weird. Nobody quite believed that it was possible, but nobody was ready to write her off, as had been the case a few years earlier when she had sailed into town from France with a wild look in her eyes. The wildness was gone, but there was definitely something in there. Others had seen it, and so had I.

But India was still not ready for such a revolutionary outlook on the way science could be – or should be – conducted. The public-private approach would have to wait. Forced into a decision at this crossroads, Villoo decided she would go hell-bent for leather along the private road. She registered her company as Avestha Gengraine Technologies (Avesthagen for short), moved out of UAS and rented a small bungalow in Bangalore. She hired a financial controller and wrote a business plan.

Attracting capital venture was the next step and it was a struggle. Somehow, between 1999 and 2001, Villoo managed to attract a substantial amount of interest from a wide variety of people. She had long believed that only through an international focus would biotech emerge as the powerhouse it could become in India. She pushed ahead, far faster than many of her supporters would have wanted, but it's hard to harness a ripening pomegranate and no one could slow her down. The next thing anyone knew, she had leased an entire floor in Bangalore's spanking new world-class International Technology Park. She even managed to rope in Dr. S.M. Krishna, Karnataka's vivacious chief minister (and yet another maverick), to inaugurate the lab. She called me one day in mid-March and asked me to fly down from Hyderabad to photograph the event, which of course I did. Dr. Krishna cut the ribbon on March 21, 2001.

About the same time, ICRISAT asked me to return to the institute to head their new public awareness programme. I accepted. Almost immediately, Villoo was banging on the door. This time it was different. A new director general was in charge, and this one was far more amenable to unusual or unprecedented tie-ups with the private sector. In no time at all, Villoo set up a small company on the campus. To manage it, she recruited Koen Wentink, who, like Villoo, had been a research scholar at ICRISAT during the early 80s. Koen was to become a key investor in Avesthagen.

Villoo had long believed that only through an international focus would biotech emerge as the powerhouse it could become in India.

During the first decade of the new century, Avesthagen grew from strength to strength. The company developed four business units – bio-pharmaceuticals, bio-agriculture, bio-nutrition and scientific innovation – all of which are on track to achieve all the expectations laid out in the company's business plan.

During this period, Villoo and her company were accorded an array of awards, perhaps none so fitting as Avesthagen's distinction as Red Herring 100 Asia Winner 2006 for Disruptive Innovation. This writer can imagine no description more appropriate for Villoo herself than that of a 'disruptive innovator'! Her most impressive award is the *Officier de l'Ordre National du Mérite*, which was bestowed on her by no less than Nikolas Sarkozy, the then President of France, in 2008. In late 2005, after over 16 years in India, I accepted a post in Dubai. It was hard to leave India and so many good friends, not least Villoo and her wonderful family. But when she contacted me a few years later to set up a meeting with biotech entrepreneurs and the scientific community in that middle-eastern boom town, I once again fell under the narcotic influence of the Pomegranate Kid, who had by this time been fully nurtured and was dropping seeds everywhere she went. Her presentation and business meetings went swimmingly, and Dubai remains a target for Avesthagen business initiatives.

In 2007, my family returned to India. It was great to visit old friends, but the principle reason for scheduling the visit in August was to attend the wedding of Villoo's elder daughter, Farah. It was not an ordinary wedding. Farah was married in traditional Parsi style at the magnificent Maharaja's Palace in Bangalore, which Villoo had rented for the occasion. Farah's bridegroom, however, was not a Parsi. Pierre Socha, Avesthagen's Vice President, Corporate Strategy, is French. Villoo found a senior Parsi priest, who believes, as she does, that unless Parsis started marrying outside of their closed community, their exquisite culture is doomed. Leave it to Villoo to extend her innovative, untrammelled generosity of spirit to matters as close to the heart as her religion and her family.

This generosity of spirit is exemplified by The Avesthagenome Project, a serious scientific venture that is unlikely to earn Villoo a single rupee in the near term. The project seeks to build a genealogical and medical database of the Parsis, an endogamous community, in order to establish linkage between genes, diseases and environmental factors, leading to the capability of predicting diseases and developing new therapies and diagnostics.

Villoo's company, Avesthagen, represents the culmination of the aspirations and hard work of a dedicated team, which at its peak consisted of over 700 employees, of which 350 were involved in research and development. Prior to 2008, Avesthagen's strategic fund and equity fund raised nearly $50 million. However in the wake of the global meltdown after 2008, Villoo had to make some hard decisions. Avesthagen had been poised to go public and in fact, had already announced its initial public offering (IPO) when the financial meltdown hit. Faced with this dilemma, many companies would have simply bit the dust. But the Avesthagen team, led by the indefatigable Villoo Morawala-Patell, demonstrated its resilience by transitioning into active commercialization and changing its primary focus from research and development to strategic product development. Another idea was of monetizing Avesthagen's intangible assets of intellectual property – perhaps the first company in India to do so.

The process of rebuilding has now endured for six years. Fearlessly looking for an innovative growth engine to embrace the new realities, Villoo brought back Avesthagen's original discovery and development model. Moreover, the restructuring of the company's products into three separate subsidiaries has enabled each one to proceed with strategic partners. The innovative Avesthagenome Project will stand for decades as a novel biomarker, and Avesthagen's unique capabilities and experience will lead the way towards the development of environmentally adjusted crops with markers for tolerance for drought and salinity as well as enhanced nutrition.

Many times, when people rise from modest circumstances to positions of prominence and power, their admirers tell how they fought through the opposition to achieve their ends. But Villoo's achievements have left no wreckage behind. In her pursuit of success, she has carried her team along with her without leaving scars. It is true that she has been opposed, that some jealous people have regretted her success, that some have tried to short-circuit her path to the top. But rather than stopping to fight these 'nay-sayers', Villoo chose to ignore them to get on with the business at hand. She simply had better things to do. Pomegranates are like that.

Early in this story, I had mentioned that Villoo's family and mine would both be involved in a second Parsi ceremony, the first being Sanaya's *navjot*. Now, it was Sanaya's turn for a fairytale wedding, this time at the Falaknuma Palace in Hyderabad, the Nizam's 110-year-old palace that had just been overhauled by the Taj Group into a luxury hotel. And the bridegroom? Well, it was that same little boy who attended Sanaya's *navjot*, my own son Tucker. This marriage has inextricably entwined Villoo's family and mine, something for which I am most grateful.

Part and parcel of Villoo's long-range vision was to prepare for the future of Avesthagen. Both of her daughters, Farah and Sanaya, have successfully defended their PhD theses at Cambridge University, and Sanaya has taken a prominent role on the board of the company. What's more? Both have given birth to the next generation of pomegranates.

In her pursuit of success, Villoo has carried her team along with her without leaving scars.

Villoo's efforts to create something *by*, *of*, and *for* her beloved India, will doubtless be rewarded by success. As she says, "We believe in the need for Avesthagen for India and we must continue and will do so. Good days are around the corner."

Through the years, the pomegranate has been nurtured by enlightened administrators, scientists and businesspeople. But in the final analysis, the fruit was ripened by Villoo herself – through hard work, a high level of intelligence, a deep and abiding compassion for others, and a refreshing nobility of spirit.

The smouldering fire in Villoo's eyes is still there. It is not always apparent, but it's always alive... ready for something new, ready to burn away the fogs of complacency and mediocrity.

You have not heard the last of the Pomegranate Kid.

Note: Much of the background material for this story was gleaned from an in-depth interview with Villoo in the July 19, 2007 issue of Money Life, and the book *Pathbreakers II*, by Sucheta Dalal and Debashish Basu – an Indian personal finance magazine, as part of a series on 'Inspiring Success Stories'.

Biographer

Eric McGaw was always passionate about the written word. His penchant for writing has always delighted and informed those who read his works, turning what would otherwise be a rather mundane topic into something captivating and unforgettable. He was a pivotal figure in several international communities and organizations whose work still influences those few industries he was involved with. A few of his accolades include the Silver award for Writing from Agricultural Communicators in Education (ACE) for the series 'Food from Thought', Gold award for Four Color Special Report from ACE for the International Crops Research Institute for the Semi-Arid Tropics (ICRISAT) Southern and Eastern Africa Region Annual Report 1995, and the author of *Improving the Unimprovable*, ICRISAT's successful nomination for the King Baudouin Award 1996. Sadly, Eric McGaw passed away in March 2016. He leaves behind a loving wife, two sons and a daughter.

moJOsh Inspirator Power 21:
The Power of Individual Social Responsibility – ISR
(Includes Team Spirit, Loyalty, Accountable Citizenship)

"We know only too well that what we are doing is nothing more than a drop in the ocean. But if the drop were not there, the ocean would be missing something."

~ Mother Theresa

Thought Leadership for Reflection: The mantra is "I change to change India, I change to change the world." Each of us has the power to "be the change", like the people featured in *Karma Kurry* Book 1 and 2.

Ideas for Action: Having **Individual Social Responsibility,** meaning having the sense that you need to take responsibility for your own contribution to the well-being of humanity, environment, world, nation, social groups and community you participate and live in. Remember: "I cannot change everything, but I can change something and if I have the integrity to do so then I would inspire others to join in and become part of the team who are loyal and accountable citizens."

Acknowledgements

To me, this is possibly the dearly important part of my books. The part where I get to express gratitude and acknowledge my family, friends, mentors, teachers and siblings, who have a made a huge difference in my life and inspired me continuously to unleash my potential. Some have been directly involved in my life and the stories and learning that I share in my books and leadership talks and workshops and others who have indirectly been with me in my journey of life and heroic storytelling.

Here's offering my sincere, heartfelt thanks to:

My mother: Betty Lucia Martins for her strength of character and courage of conviction.

My wife Jugnu Grewal Almeida for being my inspiration through thick and thin, her mother Malkit "Mini" Grewal, father Col. Randhir "Gary" Grewal, sister Kimmy Grewal Dhanoa, our nephew Karan Dhanoa and his life partner Mehak Gupta along with her parents Seema and Gopal Gupta for being an integral and energizing part of my family and life.

My sisters and brothers with their significant others: Effie and her life partner Elwin, Liza and her life partner Cassius,

Achilles (Archie) and his life partner Neha, and Vivian (Maverick) for all their love they shower on me.

My Sons: Zorawar Wilfred Singh Almeida and Ransher Wilfred Singh Almeida for being constant inspirations and reminders to do my bit to create a better world for future generations.

My nieces and nephew: Elisa, Emily and Ethan

My family members: Aunty & Uncles - Wilson Almeida, Orson Almeida and Nelin Almeida, and Cousins - Sakina and Ashley Torquato, Tracy and Edwin Pinto, Bidisha and Kyron Almeida, Geetu and Terry Almeida, for being there in my life.

My close friends and fellow lifelong learners over the years: Savio Desa, who was my closest and oldest buddy; Amin Pawar, Rex Fernandes and Wilfred Desa, who have been dear and near friends for over three decades; Anurag Nirbhaya, who has been a pillar of strength for over 20 years; Radhika and Kapil Dhall, with whom I have great moments of sharing; Anil Puri, with whom I share and gain entrepreneurial insights; Darab Talyarkhan, who has been a great friend and mentor; Freddy Mendonca, who overwhelms me with his affection; Alfred Arambhan, who is a fountain of learning; Celita Kizlibash and Vivek Paul, who volunteered to work without any conditions to make *Karma Kurry* into a TV series; and all my learning partners for the *Karma Kurry* and moJOsh Inspirator research: Aditi Misra, Advik Upadhyaya, Aditya Ahluwalia, Akhil Shahani, Alicia Ingty, Arvinder Reen, Armando Gonsalves, Aman Vaidya, Amar Agrawal, Ananya Nanda, Anil Nakhasi, Anurag Batra, Avinash Anand Singh, Bakhtawar Brar, Bidisha Paul, Bill Drayton, Digraj Singh, Eitu Vij Chopra, Gaurav Mishra, Gautam Nanda, Gregory Roberts, Hariharan Iyer, Harshit Sehdev, Hunar Brar, Hubert

Gomes, Madhu Bhatnagar, Mallika Puri, Manika Sharma, Manish Bhatnagar, Mark Parkinson, Meenu Chopra, Michael Norton, Mitu Khurana, Monica Auluck Sagar, Nilanjana Biswas, Nipun Malhotra, Preeti Monga, Rashmi Anand, Ricardo Rebello, Rishabh Bhatnagar, Roshni Shenazz, Sailesh Mishra, Sanjeev Dutta, Saurav Purkayastha, P. Sridhar Reddy, Sunny Jorawar Singh, Tarun Chauhan, Uttara Singh, Varun Khanna, Vinay Gupta and all others who have contributed in my journey of learning.

My mentors and teachers who had a big impact in my life: Benny, Joan Soares, Renee Carvalho, Fleur Almeida, Manuel Raphael, Alex Fernandes, Stephen Covey, Harsh Mander, Richard Saul Wurman, Richard (Dick) McHugh, John Grinder, Daniel Goleman, Phil Zimbardo, Venkat Pulla, S. Parasuraman and Suni Didi (Sunita is a sex worker from Kamathipura, whom I met when I was 17 while volunteering with the sex workers), who was the first to tell me at that time that I should get into teaching as she saw my calling much before I did.

All my old friends and school buddies from the class of 1986 at St. Xavier's high school, Fort, Bombay (because we are the best, better than all the rest).

My mentor and the Indian People's President Dr. APJ Abdul Kalam, who after reading *Karma Kurry 1*, offered to be our ambassador for the International Volunteering Olympiad through which we shall be taking the *Karma Kurry* stories and moJOsh Inspirator Leadership and Life lessons to schools, parents, teachers and the students all around India.

My friends at Team Jaico: Ashwin Shah and Akash Shah for all their efforts to promote the Karma Kurry Franchise, Sandhya Iyer and her team for their brilliant editing and shaping of the book, Vijay Thakur for his amazing marketing efforts and everyone else at Jaico for all their inexorable efforts to make *Karma Kurry* a successful mission. A special mention here for the former editor at Jaico, Late Mr. Rayasam Sharma, who got me started with Jaico for the *Karma Kurry* book series.

All our **Karmaveer Puraskaar** award recipients and **Rex Karmaveer Global Fellows** from over the past 10 years, from whom we have drawn huge inspiration and learning to create the *Karma Kurry* stories and moJOsh Inspirator leadership and life lessons. (Some of you are featured in this book. Thank you, for your stories and a special thanks to all the biographers)… and the best for the last,

All my readers and friends who have drawn inspiration from the true stories of real heroes in *Karma Kurry*. We are because of all of you.

So, thank you everybody (which includes everyone who has touched my life and may not be listed here), for all your inspiration and encouragement.

Keep shining bright like the stars that you are, by continuously unleashing your UNLIMITED heroic potential.

In Gratitude with Love.

Jeroninio

JAICO PUBLISHING HOUSE
Elevate Your Life. Transform Your World.

ESTABLISHED IN 1946, Jaico Publishing House is home to world-transforming authors such as Sri Sri Paramahansa Yogananda, Osho, The Dalai Lama, Sri Sri Ravi Shankar, Robin Sharma, Deepak Chopra, Jack Canfield, Eknath Easwaran, Devdutt Pattanaik, Khushwant Singh, John Maxwell, Brian Tracy and Stephen Hawking.

Our late founder Mr. Jaman Shah first established Jaico as a book distribution company. Sensing that independence was around the corner, he aptly named his company Jaico ('Jai' means victory in Hindi). In order to service the significant demand for affordable books in a developing nation, Mr. Shah initiated Jaico's own publications. Jaico was India's first publisher of paperback books in the English language.

While self-help, religion and philosophy, mind/body/spirit, and business titles form the cornerstone of our non-fiction list, we publish an exciting range of travel, current affairs, biography, and popular science books as well. Our renewed focus on popular fiction is evident in our new titles by a host of fresh young talent from India and abroad. Jaico's recently established Translations Division translates selected English content into nine regional languages.

Jaico's Higher Education Division (HED) is recognized for its student-friendly textbooks in Business Management and Engineering which are in use countrywide.

In addition to being a publisher and distributor of its own titles, Jaico is a major national distributor of books of leading international and Indian publishers. With its headquarters in Mumbai, Jaico has branches and sales offices in Ahmedabad, Bangalore, Bhopal, Bhubaneswar, Chennai, Delhi, Hyderabad, Kolkata and Lucknow.

www.ingramcontent.com/pod-product-compliance
Lightning Source LLC
Chambersburg PA
CBHW022122080426
42734CB00006B/217